Git Essentials - A Developer's Guide to Git

StackAbuse

Git Essentials - A Developer's Guide to Git

StackAbuse

Leanpub

This is a Leanpub book. Leanpub empowers authors and publishers with the Lean Publishing process. Lean Publishing is the act of publishing an in-progress ebook using lightweight tools and many iterations to get reader feedback, pivot until you have the right book and build traction once you do.

Contents

1. Introduction to Git

Git Essentials - Developer's Guide to Git is a book for everyone, beginner to advanced in software engineering, written to get you up to speed with the world's most prevalent *version control system*. Git has become *synonymous* with *Version Control Systems* (VCSs) and is expected to be under the belt of every developer as one of the most basic tools used to coordinate software development.

Oftentimes, developers aren't fully acquainted with Git but, due to its simplicity in certain areas, it's easy to work with some basic operations without really understanding what's going on. This more often than not leads to constant searching for commands, browsing StackOverflow and Google endlessly, and ultimately confusion when the answers use terms that aren't as beginner-friendly as some of the basic commands are.

The book assumes no prior experience with Git and applies to all languages and operating systems. It covers everything you need to know, from why version control systems are considered fundamental tools and the basics of Git to advanced operations with best practices and a printable PDF cheat sheet to encapsulate all of that content in an easy-to-lookup list of common commands, tasks and errors you'll use in your day-to-day career.

Though Git is not a tool exclusively reserved for developers, this book has been written and edited by developers and with a technical target audience in mind. However, if you're not alienated from opening a terminal (or console) and wish to learn about Git - you're more than welcome!

So what can you expect to do after reading this book?

- Knowledge of Version Control Systems.
- Setting up Git on your local machine.
- Knowledge of Git-related concepts.
- Knowledge of both basic and advanced Git operations.
- Ability to collaborate on a Git repository with branches, remote repositories, and branching models.
- Ability to organize your work efficiently with Git.
- Knowledge to avoid common dangers and pitfalls.

Throughout the book, we'll be building a very simple project to help out with illustrating the workings of Git. The final state of that example can be found on GitHub[1], an immensely popular platform for hosting software engineering projects and version control using Git.

We'll be using Java to create a simple calculator, though, the exact same steps are applied to any type of file or language you're using. Whether you're writing a fantasy book and want to keep track of the changes, or you're making software - Git applies to all in much the same way.

The book is written and meant to be read from start to end, since it aims at readers without much or small prior experience with Git, though, feel free to skip any chapters you're already familiar with if you feel confident about your knowledge.

---

[1]https://github.com/dupirefr/calculator

2. Source Code Management - SCM

What is Source Code Management?

A good question to begin with would be:

What is Source Code Management?

Source Code Management could be defined as the process of tracking modifications in the code of a software solution. It's worth noting that *Source Code Management* and *Version Control* refer to the same thing. You'll come across *"SCM"*, *"VCS"*, *"Source Control"*, *"Version Control"*, *"Revision Control"*, etc. interchangeably, in the context of software development.

Version Control itself, can also have a broader meaning - controlling the versions or changes of anything. A curious use case of Version Control Systems would be keeping track of changes in the legislation and laws of a country.

In robust systems, where even small changes can impact a lot of other modules, keeping track of them is paramount. Knowing who made the change, with a timestamp associated with it, and a clear view of what was changed would be able to change the way we bring about laws.

It's not unheard of for legislators of to debate wrong law proposals, and only realizing that they're discussing an outdated version after wasting valuable time, simply because the documents given to them and the changes made to them weren't tracked properly.

The same type of issue can be seen in software development - a single line of code, or rather, even a single character in one module can cause a lot of issues in a related module, or due to a chain-reaction, even unrelated modules, in a robust system.

People can spend a lot of time debating, fixing and debugging the software, losing valuable time, simply because they can't *revert* the change that broke the codebase.

It's not about singling out and persecuting the entity that made the change - it's about having the flexibility of going forward, backward, and patching pieces of software in a way that allows an entire team of people to more easily communicate and work together.

It was exactly this kind of scenario that lead to the first Source Code Management system, back in 1972.

The problem was evident - imagine a server with production code, and a few developers with their own machines, downloading a copy of the code from the server before adding new features and fixing bugs.

In the best case, they were each working one at a time on a given, specified file, and merged everything back with making changes that don't change the output for other modules. In this happy scenario, they just had to make their changes, upload the file back on the server, and they were done. Everything works, given a good amount of coordination before starting to work on the code.

> Now, a more probable scenario would be - multiple people committing changes to the same files as other developers at the same time.

What happened then was that the developers working on the same files entered, without even knowing it, a competition in which the last one to upload their version of the files to the server wins. Indeed, their version would replace the existing files, throwing away the changes the other developers, who finished their work first, made.

The problems here were:

- A developer working on the same file as another one, without knowing it.
- The absence of a mechanism of some kind to prevent overriding changes that were made simultaneously.

Those lead to the creation of the first source code management system known as: *SCCS (Source Code Control System).*

This proprietary tool was created by Marc Rochkind at IBM in 1972. It established the foundation of more modern VCSs.

What is Git?

Though time, many systems addressing this exact problem were made. One of them was Git, a very popular VCS used by a large population of developers across the world.

A Brief History of Git

Git was created in 2005 by Linus Torvalds. Its purpose was to replace the version control system used at that time to manage the Linux kernel sources, which wasn't open source and presented a few drawbacks to the community working on the kernel. Additionally, the tool was no longer free to use at that time.

As no other VCSs were matching the needs of the community, Torvalds decided to write his own. 10 years after its creation, Torvaldis had an interview[2] regarding Git and how far it's come in the trailing decade, in which he further explains why Git was born and which issues they faced before making that decision.

How Does Git Work?

Git is known to be a *distributed version control system*. In opposition to a *centralized VCS*, a distributed VCS doesn't keep the history of modifications of the source code in a single centralized repository, but rather keeps a filesystem copy on each developer's computer - meaning every developer that cloned the project has the full history stored on their own hard drive.

There are advantages and disadvantages to using a distributed VCS. The advantages are mostly linked to the fact that most operations carried on a distributed VCS are local:

- **Operations are fast**, except those involving exchanges with distant servers. Most of the operations you'll perform will be on your local machine. At the end of the day, week, or month, you'll *push* all the changes to the distant servers.
- It's possible to **work without a network access** without losing the possibility to divide that work into a meaningful, separate, unit of change.

---

[2]https://www.linuxfoundation.org/blog/2015/04/10-years-of-git-an-interview-with-git-creator-linus-torvalds

- The developers can privately and locally track work if they want to try out things without impacting others. This allows you to be as creative as you'd like, thinking outside the box and testing things out, without dragging anyone down or complicating it for others. Of course, since everything is eventually merged into one project, this is no excuse not to follow the same standards and conventions as others.

Git has tackled this task by creating 2 areas - *local* and *remote*. The *local* area additionally has three areas - *working directory*, *staging area* and *local repository*.

A *repository* is just a directory that Git is looking over, keeping track of the changes within it.

When you're working on code, you start out in the *working directory*. You'll typically alter the contents of files through an IDE and run your code. Once you're happy with a change you've made, you can *add* the changed files to the *staging area*. The staging area is basically just the area that's waiting to be *committed* as a change. Before being committed, changes aren't timestamped. Once you add a file to the staging area, if you alter it again, it'll become *unstaged* again.

You can alter files many times, add them to the staging area, and then once you have a cohesive "step" you'd like to "engrave", you *commit* the files from the staging area to the *local repository*.

The local repository is your local copy of the remote repository you're working on with other people. Once you've got a stable build that you're happy with, you can then *push* your local changes to the *remote* repository.

We'll go over all of these concepts in detail and practice in the upcoming chapters.

Additionally, the way that Git works is that it captures data in terms of *snapshots*. It doesn't *keep track of changes*, it keeps entire files and their states in full. Once you change a file and *commit the change* (make it persistent, i.e. *snapshot* it), the new state is registered and saved, alongside other files. If you change that same file again, and commit the change - you'll have three versions of that file. You'll have the original file, the same file with the first change, and the same file with the second change.

If you don't commit any changes to a file, it's not stored again, and you simply have a reference to the latest snapshot:

Version 1	Version 2	Version 3
File 1 (state 1)	File 1 (state 1)	File 1 (state 1)
File 2 (state 1)	File 2 (state 2)	File 2 (state 3)
File 3 (state 1)	File 3 (state 1)	File 3 (state 2)

In this scenario, *File 1* was never changed. It maintained it state throughout three versions. Though, *File 2* has been altered multiple times. *File 3* was altered once after *Version 1*.

Each of these files now have their own history of sorts, and that history spans through different versions of the project.

Each of these snapshots/states will be accessible on something you might imagine as a temporal slider. You can go back and forth with these versions as much as you'd like. It's exactly as if you can turn back time to a previous snapshot if you'd like to take a step back. And of course, you're not confined to jumping entire versions either. You can go back into the history of *File 1* a bit, back into *state 1*, but leave the other two files in their respective states in *Version 3*.

This feature can also become a disadvantage, to a degree. When it comes to dealing with large files, having the full history of those files modifications can be space consuming. It might not sound like a lot, but having huge files, with hundreds of committed changes by team members produces a big file history.

And, even if the files are not that big, having a large history might take long to download, though, since we've gone a long way to improve storage technologies and memories, disk space isn't a really big issue.

On the other hand, various VCS' don't keep entire file histories like this, but rather only keep the differences in files tracked. If a file has 100 lines, and you make a change on line 50, only that single line change is registered and when you *pull* the latest version from the system, the change is applied to the unchanged rest of the file.

Git Popularity

Git, as of 2019, holds approximately 70% of the search interests for the 5 most popular VCSs. This means that we'll find plenty of resources to help us in learning and using Git, as well as help online from other users.

Indeed, compared to other VCS like Mercurial and Subversion, Git is far more popular on the well-known computer science oriented Q&A website StackOverflow: 125K questions[3] for Git against 23k questions[4] and 8k questions[5] for Subversion and Mercurial, respectively.

---

[3] https://stackoverflow.com/questions/tagged/git
[4] https://stackoverflow.com/questions/tagged/svn
[5] https://stackoverflow.com/questions/tagged/mercurial

RhodeCode published an analysis of VCS popularity[6] back in 2016, which further goes to show the shift from Subversion to Git in the modern day and age.

Additionally, as of August 2019, Git also holds around 70% of the repositories hosted for both personal and enterprise development, according to Open Hub[7], with the next largest VCS being Subversion holding ~20% of the share.

The same trend can be seen on Google's trend-tracking service Google Trends:

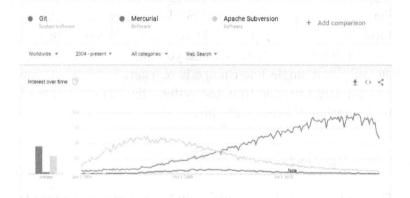

Finally, https://github.com[8], a famous platform for holding public and private Git repositories, reached the number of 100 million repositories in late 2018[9].

---

[6]https://rhodecode.com/insights/version-control-systems-2016#:~:text=sum%20this%20up%3A-,Git%20is%20the%20most%20popular%20version%20control%20system%20in%202016,Mozilla%2C%20Nginx%2C%20and%20NetBeans

[7]https://www.openhub.net/repositories/compare

[8]GitHub

[9]https://github.blog/2018-11-08-100m-repos/

3. Getting Started with Git

Now's the time to get started with our first steps in using Git. First of all, we'll install it on Windows, MacOS and Linux, depending on your personal preference. Then, we'll configure it with some basic configurations, such as specifying which user we are to avoid retyping the credentials on each operation that requires authorization. Finally, we'll create a new file and *commit* it to our *repository*!

Installing Git

First, let's install Git on our computer. The three following sections explain how to do it on Windows, Mac OS, and Linux, respectively. Feel free to jump right to your favorite operating system.

> **Please note**: The version used throughout this book is **2.30.0.**, which was released on the 28th of December, 2020. As significant releases of the tool get pushed, we'll update the book as necessary.

Windows

To install Git on Windows, we'll navigate to the official git-scm[10] website's download page. Depending on your system,

---

[10]https://git-scm.com/download/win

you can choose a portable or regular setup file. We'll go with
the adequate version of the regular setup file.

Once downloaded, we can run the exe file. Then, a wizard will
guide us through the installation step by step. We'll go with
the default options here.

Once finished, Git should be installed and situated on your
PC. Now, using the Command Prompt, or the Git Bash[11] application, you can run the git command, with the --version
flag to check the installed version:

```
1   $ git --version
```

It should output something along the lines of:

```
1   git version 2.30.0.windows.1
```

You might have a different version installed, depending on the
time you're reading this book, and the latest stable release at
that point in time.

If you're used to working with the Command Prompt, it's
fully valid to use the Command Prompt for Git. If you're
used to running a bash environment, such as working with
Linux, you might be more comfortable with the Git Bash
application, as it also allows you to use most of the standard
Unix commands that Windows doesn't have natively.

Git Bash additionally has more contrasting and customized
highlighting and contains some information that isn't shown
in the Command Prompt.

---

[11]https://gitforwindows.org/

MacOS

A few options are available to install Git on a MacOS computer. The first one is using Homebrew[12]. We can install it if it's not already done. Then, we can run the following command in a terminal:

```
1   $ brew install git
```

Another option is to use the installer provided by Tim Harper[13]. We just have to download it and use the default options.

Once installed, check the version:

```
1   $ git --version
```

It should output something along the lines of:

```
1   git version 2.30.0
```

Linux

Installing Git on Linux really depends of our distribution, and its underlying package manager. We'll consider a Debian-based distribution here, and thus, use the apt-get command-line tool:

```
1   $ apt-get install git
```

Once installed, we can run the familiar command again:

---

[12]https://brew.sh/
[13]https://sourceforge.net/projects/git-osx-installer/

```
1  $ git --version
```

It should output something along the lines of:

```
1  git version 2.30.0
```

Basic Setup

Now that we've installed Git, we can start using it. Well, almost! We'll want to set up a user name and email for Git.

To do that, let's open a terminal and run two commands:

```
1  $ git config --global user.name francois
2  $ git config --global user.email francois.dupire@ne\
3  rthusconsulting.be
```

What happened here?

Both of these commands start with the `git` keyword, which is typical. You'll access all of the Git commands in this book using exactly this keyword. Then, we've passed the `config` operation.

As the name implies, we've told Git that we'll be dabbling with the configuration now. It's worth noting that Git has *local* and *global* configuration files.

The *local* configuration file can be found in the project (*repository*) you're working with. These configurations override the global ones and are usually used if you want to set up some configurations specifically for a single project. By default, all configuration changes made by `git config` are local. This file is situated under the .git directory in your project. You can access it via .git/config. We'll talk about this folder once we've started working on a project.

You have to specify the --global flag explicitly to make changes to the global configuration. This file is situated outside of your projects, usually under ~/.gitconfig on Linux, $HOME/.gitconfig on MacOS and C:/Users/User/.gitconfig on Windows.

The values in this configuration file apply to all Git repositories/projects you're keeping track of using Git, unless they're overridden by a local file in a repository/project.

Both files accept key-value pairs of configuration statements. For example, we've set the user.name key to be francois in our first command. After that, we've set user.email to francois.dupire@nerthusconsulting.be.

If you'd like to, at any point, check which configurations apply to a specific project - while you're in that project's directory, you can run the following command:

```
1  $ git config --list
```

This will list all the configurations currently being applied to the project, including both global and local configurations. This can look something along the lines of:

```
1   core.autocrlf=true
2   core.fscache=true
3   color.diff=auto
4   color.status=auto
5   color.branch=auto
6   color.interactive=true
7   help.format=html
8   http.sslcainfo=[PATH]
9   diff.astextplain.textconv=astextplain
10  rebase.autosquash=true
11  credential.helper=manager
12  filter.lfs.clean=git-lfs clean -- %f
13  filter.lfs.smudge=git-lfs smudge -- %f
14  filter.lfs.process=git-lfs filter-process
15  filter.lfs.required=true
16  user.name=francois
17  user.email=francois.dupire@nerthusconsulting.be
18  core.repositoryformatversion=0
19  core.filemode=false
20  core.bare=false
21  core.logallrefupdates=true
22  core.symlinks=false
23  core.ignorecase=true
24  remote.origin.url=[REMOTE ORIGIN URL]
25  remote.origin.fetch=+refs/heads/*:refs/remotes/orig\
26  in/*
27  branch.master.remote=origin
28  branch.master.merge=refs/heads/master
```

Though, it's unclear which configurations come from which
configuration file. We *know* that we set the user.name and
user.email in the global file, but that's where our certainty
ends.

If you'd like to check from *where* these configurations are being read, if you want to change some, for example, you can add the `--show-origin` flag:

```
1  $ git config --list --show-origin
```

This will now also include the location to the configuration file that brings about the configurations you see:

```
1   file:~/.gitconfig          filter.lfs.clean=git-lfs cl\
2   ean -- %f
3   file:~/.gitconfig          filter.lfs.smudge=git-lfs s\
4   mudge -- %f
5   file:~/.gitconfig          filter.lfs.process=git-lfs \
6   filter-process
7   file:~/.gitconfig          filter.lfs.required=true
8   file:~/.gitconfig          user.name=francois
9   file:~/.gitconfig          user.email=francois.dupire@\
10  nerthusconsulting.be
11  file:.git/config           core.repositoryformatversio\
12  n=0
13  file:.git/config           core.filemode=false
14  file:.git/config           core.bare=false
```

Great! Now we know which configuration levels are affecting our options if we need to change them at any point.

Hello, Git!

We're finally ready! Let's do it then, perform the well known "Hello World!", or rather "Hello, Git!", here! Let's create a repository, and commit a change to it.

First of all, let's create a directory that'll become our repository, and go into that directory:

```
1  $ mkdir getting-started-with-git
2  $ cd getting-started-with-git
```

And now, we'll initialize our very first Git repository:

```
1  $ git init
```

That command outputs the following:

```
1  Initialized empty Git repository in /home/francois/\
2  getting-started-with-git/.git/
```

We've *initialized* an empty Git repository. The directory now
has another .git directory within it. This directory will
contain all metadata to keep track of your project and perform
version control. This is exactly the directory that has a config
file for your project, as well as the history for all the files,
committed changes we made, etc.

By default, it'll contain:

```
1   $ cd .git
2   $ ls -la
3   total 15
4
5   drwxr-xr-x 1 dupir 197121    0 Jan 11 02:00 ./
6   drwxr-xr-x 1 dupir 197121    0 Jan 11 02:00 ../
7   -rw-r--r-- 1 dupir 197121   23 Jan 11 02:00 HEAD
8   -rw-r--r-- 1 dupir 197121  130 Jan 11 02:00 config
9   -rw-r--r-- 1 dupir 197121   73 Jan 11 02:00 descript\
10  ion
11  drwxr-xr-x 1 dupir 197121    0 Jan 11 02:00 hooks/
12  drwxr-xr-x 1 dupir 197121    0 Jan 11 02:00 info/
13  drwxr-xr-x 1 dupir 197121    0 Jan 11 02:00 objects/
14  drwxr-xr-x 1 dupir 197121    0 Jan 11 02:00 refs/
```

The config file contains configuration options. The description file contains the description of the repository/project for a web page pertaining to your project. The HEAD file contains the reference to the current branch you're on. Since this might be a tiny bit confusing without further knowledge of what branches are and how they work, we won't focus on this file right now and leave it for the oncoming chapters.

Some terminal emulators will also output the word master between parentheses next to the current path.
master is the default branch name. Again, we'll have plenty of time talking about branches later, so let's not put too much focus on that now.

So, that's a bit disappointing, we've not had the chance to say "Hello" yet. Let's do that now. First, let's create a hello.txt file with a *"Hello, Git!"* sentence in it:

```
1  $ echo "Hello, Git!" > hello.txt
```

Then, let's run the following commands:

```
1  $ git add hello.txt
2  $ git commit -m "Initial commit: sayin' hello"
```

This should output something like this:

```
1  [master (root-commit) 00ccc8c] Initial commit: sayi\
2  n' hello
3   1 file changed, 1 insertion(+)
4   create mode 100644 hello.txt
```

That's it, our first commit containing our hello.txt file! We've created a file, *added* it to our *staging area*, and *committed* that change to the *local repository*. That's a lot of both unknown commands, as well as terminology.

We'll have a closer look at them in the next chapter, with explanations for each one in detail. For now, it's enough to simply state that we've committed to persisting a change in the hello.txt file.

4. The Basics of Git

Now that we've installed git and configured some of the basic options - we can learn how to use it. We've briefly gone over the creation of a repository in the last chapter, as well as creating a file, adding it to the staging area and committing the change. To understand what was going on under the hood, we'll need to navigate through the concepts of the *repository*, *index*, *staging area* and *commits*, also mentioned briefly in Chapter 2.

Armed with those, we'll already have a working knowledge of Git, and thus will be able to use it to keep track of changes made in small projects.

Demo Project

To help us out with visualizing what's going on, we'll make use of a small demo project. We're going to implement a simple `Calculator` class in Java, and use this project throughout the book.

Don't fear if you don't know a single thing about programming in Java, this will be kept quite simple, only to serve as a support for the book, and to visualize the changes. You can supplement the book with any language and any project you're working on - be it a new one or an existing project you'd like to start performing version control on.

Again, you can find this project on GitHub[14].

---

[14]https://github.com/dupirefr/calculator

Git Repositories

We've been mentioning repositories a lot in the previous chapters. They're one of the key concepts you'll have to understand to use Git. Let's once again go over what repositories are, what their structure looks like and how to create one.

Definition and Structure

> A repository is a directory managed by Git. This means Git is tracking changes in files of that directory and its sub-directories.

We can roughly say it's composed of two things: *the working tree* and *the .git directory.*

The working tree is where the work happens. It's composed of the directories and files we're actually making changes to.

The latter is where those changes are recorded, in the form of commits, the unit of work of Git (but more on that later).

The .git directory also holds the repository-specific configuration, the branches, tags, information about operations that are in progress like merge or rebase, among other things. We'll cover all those things during the course of the book. For now, it's enough to know that the .git directory contains the data required for Git to function.

Create a Repository

Last time, we've created an empty repository in a random directory. Now, let's start a repository for our Calculator project.

Let's create a directory dedicated to our Calculator project and trigger the git init command:

```
1  $ mkdir calculator
2  $ cd calculator
3  $ git init
```

This will result in:

```
1  Initialized empty Git repository in /home/francois/\
2  calculator/.git/
```

And sure enough, if we run ls, we can see the .git directory there:

```
1  $ ls -la
2
3  total 4
4  drwxr-xr-x 1 dupir 197609 0 Jan 2 20:49 ./
5  drwxr-xr-x 1 dupir 197609 0 Jan 2 20:49 ../
6  drwxr-xr-x 1 dupir 197609 0 Jan 2 20:49 .git/
```

Note: The ls -la command should be read as: "Show all the files and directories of the current directory, as a list, comprising hidden files and directories".

The ls command displays the files and directories. Thanks to the -l option it outputs them as a list. Finally, the -a option, concatenated to the previous one here, tells the command to also show hidden files and directories.

Here, it allowed us to see the .git directory. We've seen how the directory itself looks like already. It contains the critical files required for Git to do its job in regards to our working directory/tree. You won't be accessing this directory in your day-to-day work directly. Though, every command you run will affect the files inside.

For example, when you run `git add` to add a file to the staging area, the `index` file inside the `.git` directory is updated. This directory also gives Git repositories "a sense of self". Without it, Git wouldn't recognize the directory as a repository.

Running a `git` command requires you to be in a valid Git repository. And depending on the `.git` directory, it'll know which repository it's working with.

Given our `.git` directory in the `calculator` directory, we know that the repository has been initialized correctly and that Git is now tracking changes.

As for the working directory, it's empty for now (remember, it's everything besides the `.git` directory, `./` and `../` being the current and the parent directories, respectively).

Git Commits

We briefly covered Git commits before, and used the term in various places. We even *made a commit* in Chapter 3 without going much into what they are, their composition and what we can do with them.

Now, let's get familiar with *commits* - the basic building block of Git repositories.

Definition and Composition

A commit contains one or many changes in one or many files of the repository. It can vary from adding a line to a file, to removing an entire directory or adding and renaming files.

>A *commit* is a *snapshot* of your entire project, at
>that given time.

Yes, the *entire* project. Well, technically, it only stores the
changed files as separate files since it would be insanely
expensive to *actually copy* snapshots of entire projects for a
change as small as adding a dot to a README file.

This underlying mechanism is abstracted from you, so there's
no real need to concern yourself with it. It's *intended* for the
user to understand commits as snapshots of the entire project.
When you *commit* a change, you *commit* the state of the entire
project, after making some changes.

Each commit is composed of a few things:

- A unique ID, in the form of a *hash*. Each commit can
  be accessed and reviewed at any given time, unless you
  squash multiple commits into one and thus end up with
  only one.
- The author of the commit.
- The timestamp the commit was created at.
- A commit message - a user-defined message, possibly in
  multiple lines, generally holding information about the
  changes recorded in the commit.
- A reference to a previous commit (except for the first
  one, which has no previous commit to point to).
- The changes we brought (conceptually, as technically a
  copy of the changed files is referenced by a commit.

A hash is a unique representation of a single data point or a
set of data. It's calculated using hashing algorithms (such as

MD5, SHA-256, BCrypt, etc.). Those algorithms take the data as input and give back a hexadecimal string that is the hash.

The difference between *hashing* and *encryption* is that there is no decrypting a hash. Hashes are one-way functions. There are no algorithms to convert a hash back to its initial data. The same input will give the same output, and the only way to validate a hash is to feed the same original, unhashed, value to the function.

Some hash functions implement *salting*, which add a totally random *salt* to the end of the hashed string, which isn't something you can reproduce given the same input. Though, going deeper into this isn't relevant for the book.

Some usages of hashes are:

- Storing passwords or secret data safely (by hashing them).
- Transform larger data into short hashes.

In Git, the hash of a commit uniquely identifies this commit because it's generated from all the commit's data, using an SHA-1 algorithm. A commit's hash can be seen as its fingerprint. It's so unique, since it contains *all* of the commit's data - the author of the commit, the message you put in, the exact timestamp, and the *entire working tree.*

All of this is fed into an SHA-1 one-way function, and hashed into a 40-digit commit hash/id. You can rest assured that nobody, nowhere, ever will have the exact same commit hash as the one you've created. It's intrinsically tied to the work you've done and you can rest assured that when Git loads in your commit, it's the exact state your files were in when you made the commit. This is also what people mean when they say that Git has **integrity**.

As the hash is really short compared to the total amount of input data, it makes much more sense to compare commits by their hashes, instead of the input data.

Also, we can access all of this data of a commit, by providing the commit's hash to Git. We'll take a look at how to do that later this chapter.

Knowing all that, we can say that **a repository is a sequence of commits**, as illustrated in the schema below:

In the next chapter, we'll see that it's a bit more complex than that, but let's stick to that definition for now.

Recording Commits

Knowing what commits are, let's go ahead and record some commits for our project. Let's say we create a README.md file in the calculator directory to explain what our project is about:

```
1  $ touch README.md
```

Now, if we run ls -la, we'll be greeted with:

```
1   $ ls -la
2
3   total 5
4   drwxr-xr-x 1 dupir 197609 0 Jan 2 20:49 ./
5   drwxr-xr-x 1 dupir 197609 0 Jan 2 20:49 ../
6   drwxr-xr-x 1 dupir 197609 0 Jan 2 20:49 .git/
7   -rw-r--r-- 1 dupir 197609 0 Jan 2 21:49 README.md
```

The README.md file is in our working directory, but Git isn't yet aware of it since we didn't *add* it to the staging area. Let's do that:

```
1   $ git add README.md
```

And finally, let's commit it:

```
1   $ git commit -m "Initial commit"
```

If everything went well, the terminal should output something like this:

```
1   [master (root-commit) d6753cb] Initial commit
2    1 file changed, 0 insertions(+), 0 deletions(-)
3    create mode 100644 README.md
```

What can we get from this output? Well:

- The current branch, master (don't worry about branches for now, we'll cover them in the next chapter).
- The commit hash, here d6753cb. Note that this is a shortened version of the full hash, which should already allow us to uniquely identify the commit.

- The commit message, specified by `-m "Initial commit"`.
- Information about the changes - here one file has been created, but there were neither insertions nor deletions (no lines were added nor deleted).

Typically instead of the `root-commit`, you'd have a parent commit's hash there. However, since this is the first commit we've performed, `root-commit` implies the absence of a parent.

We can get more information from the `git log` command, which shows the full sequence of commits in our repository. We only have one, so it's the only one that'll show up:

```
1  commit d6753cb4d15ed30815b480fbf1c5c8abc6a63ca1 (HE\
2  AD -> master)
3  Author: francois <francois.dupire@nerthusconsulting\
4  .be>
5  Date:   Sat Jan 2 22:58:19 2021 +0100
6
7      Initial commit
```

You can see that the first 7 characters of the full commit hash are the ones we've gotten back when we made the commit.

The `git log` command is a useful one. It allows us to print the commits present on the current branch to the console.

We're going to use that command throughout the book, and discover some of its options along the way.

Here, we can see some extra information:

- The full commit hash - `9061b9d605c99bd97d`...
- The author.

- The timestamp.
- Information about the location of the commit in the sequence, here HEAD on the master branch, meaning the last commit of that branch.
- The commit message.

We could stop there, that's pretty much what we need to do to record changes to a Git repository. However, we're going to dive deeper into the underlying concepts, and we're also going to see more convenient ways to handle a larger number of files.

Index and Staging Area

First, let's discuss the concepts of the index and staging areas.

> The index is a list of the files known to (tracked by) the Git repository.

To illustrate this, let's add a line to our README.md file, and let's create an empty Calculator.java class (it's going to hold our implementation of the Calculator):

```
1  $ echo "# Calculator Project" >> README.md
2  $ echo "public class Calculator {}" >> Calculator.j\
3  ava
```

Here, we've updated the old README.md file by adding a line, and created a new file Calculator.java with the class definition.

Now, let's run the git status command, which gives us information about what changes were made in the repository since the last commit:

```
1  $ git status
```

This results in:

```
1   On branch master
2   Changes not staged for commit:
3     (use "git add <file>..." to update what will be c\
4   ommitted)
5     (use "git restore <file>..." to discard changes i\
6   n working directory)
7          modified:    README.md
8
9   Untracked files:
10    (use "git add <file>..." to include in what will \
11  be committed)
12         Calculator.java
13
14  no changes added to commit (use "git add" and/or "g\
15  it commit -a")
```

Git gives us a lot of information regarding the current state of the repository with this command. We know that we changed two things - added a line to an existing file, and created a new one with a single line.

However, we can see that Git doesn't treat these two files in the same way - The README.md file, already tracked, appears in the "Changes not staged for commit" section, while the Calculator.java file appears in the "Untracked files" section. *The latter is not yet indexed, while the former is.*

Git knows that we have a README.md file, we've already added it before and even committed it. However, Calculator.java is new. It's still unclear whether we really want to add it to the tracked files or not. It might be a log file that we don't want to track, or it might be something that's there only temporarily.

To make sure that unwanted files don't just automatically get added to the tracked file list, Git also tells us that, to include the new file in the next commit, we have to use the git add command, and thus tell it to keep track of the changes made to it henceforth.

But, it also tells us we've to do the same with the updated file in order to record that update in the next commit. So... what gives? What's the difference between tracked and untracked files if we have to run git add for both categories? Why aren't they all in the same collection?

This brings us to the second concept - *the staging area*:

> The staging area collects the changes to be recorded
> in the next commit.

Those *aren't* necessarily *all the changes* that occurred since the last commit. For example, in our case, we could add the changes made to README.md to the staging area:

```
1  $ git add README.md
```

Let's run a git status now:

```
1  On branch master
2  Changes to be committed:
3    (use "git restore --staged <file>..." to unstage)
4        modified:   README.md
5
6  Untracked files:
7    (use "git add <file>..." to include in what will \
8  be committed)
9        Calculator.java
```

Now, our README.md file is in a *"Changes to be committed"* section, meaning that the next commit we create will record the changes brought to that file.

But, not necessarily all the changes. Let's say we decide to add yet another line to that README.md file:

```
1  $ echo "This project will hold a simple implementat\
2  ion of a Calcualtor in Java" >> README.md
```

Another call to the git status command would return:

```
1   On branch master
2   Changes to be committed:
3     (use "git restore --staged <file>..." to unstage)
4         modified:   README.md
5
6   Changes not staged for commit:
7     (use "git add <file>..." to update what will be c\
8   ommitted)
9     (use "git restore <file>..." to discard changes i\
10  n working directory)
11        modified:   README.md
```

```
12
13  Untracked files:
14    (use "git add <file>..." to include in what will \
15  be committed)
16           Calculator.java
```

Calculator.java is still untracked, since we didn't add it to the staging area yet at all. But also, our README.md is listed in *both* staged and unstaged changes. Why's that so?

Again, Git tracks files and the changes done to them. We've added the file with the initial change to our staging area. The file in that state is staged. Then, we've introduced a new state for the file, without adding it. This version of the file is unstaged.

Thus, we end up with *two versions* of the same file, in Git's eyes. After adding a file to the staging area, any further modification of that files will be considered unstaged.

Unless we add the file again, invoking the git commit command won't consider that very last line we added.

Let's do it - let's commit the currently staged changes:

```
1  $ git commit -m "Added project title to the README"
```

A last call to git status would tell us there are no further staged changes, but still an unstaged one and an untracked file:

```
1   On branch master
2   Changes not staged for commit:
3     (use "git add <file>..." to update what will be c\
4   ommitted)
5     (use "git restore <file>..." to discard changes i\
6   n working directory)
7           modified:   README.md
8
9   Untracked files:
10    (use "git add <file>..." to include in what will \
11  be committed)
12          Calculator.java
13
14  no changes added to commit (use "git add" and/or "g\
15  it commit -a")
```

Furthermore, what happens when we introduce a change to the Calculator.java class? If we change README.md, even without adding that file again, a change is tracked. Git is aware that a change has been made and tells us that the file is modified, prompting us to add the newest state to the staging area before committing it.

Let's add a main() method to the Calculator.java file:

```
1   public class Calculator() {
2       public static void main(String[] args) {}
3   }
```

Now, let's run git status again:

```
1   $ git status
```

This results in:

```
1   On branch master
2   Changes not staged for commit:
3     (use "git add <file>..." to update what will be c\
4   ommitted)
5     (use "git checkout -- <file>..." to discard chang\
6   es in working directory)
7
8           modified:   README.md
9
10  Untracked files:
11    (use "git add <file>..." to include in what will \
12  be committed)
13
14          Calculator.java
15
16  no changes added to commit (use "git add" and/or "g\
17  it commit -a")
```

Last time, when we modified the README.md file in this very
same way, Git told us that it's modified and asked us to
add it again in the new state. However, it *doesn't* track
Calculator.java at all. It isn't aware of any changes in that
file. No matter what we did to it - Git won't know what's
going on.

If we renamed the file into something else, such as - CalculatorNew,
calling:

```
1   $ git status
```

Would result in:

```
1   On branch master
2   Changes not staged for commit:
3     (use "git add <file>..." to update what will be c\
4   ommitted)
5     (use "git checkout -- <file>..." to discard chang\
6   es in working directory)
7
8           modified:   README.md
9
10  Untracked files:
11    (use "git add <file>..." to include in what will \
12  be committed)
13
14          CalculatorNew.java
15
16  no changes added to commit (use "git add" and/or "g\
17  it commit -a")
```

Now, this is a violation of Java's syntax. The public class name has to match the file name, but let's put that aside for a moment.

The renaming of the file isn't tracked. Neither would the deletion be. We can replace it with a new file, and Git would be none the wiser.

This is the difference between *unstaged* and *untracked* files - unstaged files are tracked, but some of the changes within them aren't staged while untracked files aren't relevant in the eyes of Git.

The `git add` Command

Now, we've already covered the `git add` command while learning about the staging area. But it has some options to make this process easier with many files.

Let's say we want to keep track of some solution we provide in a `CHANGELOG.md` file, so that the customer can easily see what's new with each update:

```
1   $ touch CHANGELOG.md
```

Now, we want to add this file and the `README.md` line we didn't commit earlier to the staging area. With our current knowledge we would do something like this:

```
1   $ git add README.md
2   $ git add CHANGELOG.md
```

We've got only two files here, that's not much on an inconvenience. But later, on a real project, we might deal with *5, 10, 25...n* more files, and then the nightmare begins. Of course, there are ways to add multiple files at once.

First of all, we could just list every files after the `add` command:

```
1   $ git add README.md CHANGELOG.md
```

Although it does make it a bit less painful than the previous method, since it saves us from repeating the `git` keyword every time, this isn't much of a solution.

The next option is to use file globs, and match by file extension:

```
1  $ git add *.md
```

Here, we're saying to Git it should add all files with a .md extension to the staging area. We could have given multiple file globs, or a mix of files and file globs, that's not a problem at all:

```
1  $ git add *.md *.java
```

Running this command would add all of our .md and .java files to the staging area. If we run git status after this command:

```
1  $ git status
```

We'd be greeted with:

```
1  On branch master
2  Changes to be committed:
3    (use "git reset HEAD <file>..." to unstage)
4
5         new file:    CHANGELOG.md
6         new file:    Calculator.java
7         modified:    README.md
```

Now, all of our files have been added, since all of the files in our directory end with either an ' .md or .java' extension. In reality, we work with various file types, and most of the time, you don't care about choosing the files to add, and you just want to add them all to the staging area.

This can be done either by providing the -A flag, a wildcard *, or simply a . to the call:

```
1  $ git add -A
```

Or:

```
1  $ git add .
```

Or even:

```
1  $ git add *
```

This will add all the changes to the staging area, whether the files are indexed or not. We should note that these are the shortened version of the --all option.

Running either of these commands will add *all* (both tracked and untracked) files, and their latest changes to the staging area.

The git commit Command

Now that we know how to stage our files correctly and have added them all to the staging area, we can proceed with the committing part:

```
1  $ git commit -m "Extra information about the projec\
2  t, a changelog file and our future Calculator class\
3   file"
```

This command is pretty straightforward, it records the changes in the staging area into a new commit object with the message passed to the -m (or --message) flag. It also keeps track of the timestamp and author.

This results in:

```
1  [master c3bbde2] Extra information about the projec\
2  t, a changelog file and our future Calculator class\
3   file
4   3 files changed, 4 insertions(+), 1 deletion(-)
5   create mode 100644 CHANGELOG.md
6   create mode 100644 Calculator.java
```

If we don't use the message option, Git will launch an editor
for us to give a message to the commit. Let's add a line to the
CHANGELOG.md file, add it and commit it without a message:

```
1  $ echo "Initial version of the Calculator project" \
2  >> CHANGELOG.md
3  $ git add .
4  $ git commit
```

This will open up a rudimentary text editor in your terminal:

```
1  Updated changelog with first log statement
2  # Please enter the commit message for your changes. \
3   Lines starting
4  # with '#' will be ignored, and an empty message ab\
5  orts the commit.
6  # On branch master
7  # Changes to be committed:
8  #        modified:   CHANGELOG.md
```

Once you type out a commit message, you can quit this editor
with ESC+:wq+Enter (depends heavily on the editor). This will
then save the commit like it usually does with a message.

You *can* avoid adding a message, by using:

```
1   $ git commit --allow-empty-message --no-edit
```

Or, by simply setting the message to be empty:

```
1   $ git commit -m ""
```

Though, this is highly discouraged, as it's considered really bad practice. Each change should be explained when possible.

However, that's not all we can do with that command. As a matter of fact, there is an option that allows us to, partially, bypass the git add command.

This option tells Git to commit all modified and deleted files, whether they are in the staging area or not. It'll just omit untracked files, which won't be committed:

```
1   $ git commit -am "Beautiful commit with all tracked\
2     file modifications"
```

If we'd run that before adding all our files, then only the README.md file changes would've been committed, because the CHANGELOG.md and Calculator.java files were still untracked.

This is different from running:

```
1   $ git add .
2   $ git commit -m "Beautiful commit with all file mod\
3     ifications"
```

Since the git add . command would also add the untracked files. Note that the option in its shortened form can be concatenated with other options.

Ignore Files in a Repository

Finally, let's see how we can tell Git to ignore some files in a repository. The solution isn't to keep them *untracked*, where they will pop up with each `git status`. We don't want to commit them to the repository where others may have access to them, and we just want Git to *ignore* them.

This is typical for files containing credentials, log files, installed dependencies, etc. Or even for personal stuff we want to have at hand, but don't want to commit. That's what we're going to do here.

Let's add a `TODO.md` file that will hold our personal To-Do list for the project, and we'll tell Git to ignore that file.

To achieve that, we need to add a new file to our repository, named `.gitignore`. This file will contain file names and file globs to be ignored by Git. Each line in the file is a pattern. You can simply put the name of the file, in which case, since it matches fully, it'll be ignored.

You can also put in a wildcard for a specific file extension or simply all files of a subdirectory, such as `tmp/**/*`.

Let's create our file:

```
1  $ echo "* [ ] Finalize Git repository setup" >> TOD\
2  O.md
3  $ echo "* [ ] Provide an addition method in Calcula\
4  tor.java" >> TODO.md
```

If we run a `git status` command, the file will appear as untracked:

```
1  On branch master
2  Untracked files:
3    (use "git add <file>..." to include in what will \
4  be committed)
5
6          TODO.md
```

Let's now create a .gitignore file and add an entry to it:

```
1  echo "TODO.md" >> .gitignore
```

If we call git status again, here's what's shown in the terminal:

```
1  On branch master
2  Untracked files:
3    (use "git add <file>..." to include in what will \
4  be committed)
5          .gitignore
6
7  nothing added to commit but untracked files present\
8    (use "git add" to track)
```

The TODO.md file doesn't appear anymore, but the .gitignore file does! Ironically enough, the file *isn't* ignored by default. This is because, presumably, everyone in your team will want to ignore the same files as you do.

If you don't commit your .gitignore file, and someone comes up with a different list of ignored files, your project files will be in conflict. In most cases, you'll want to have your .gitignore file to be staged and committed in the repository.

While this file is reserved for Git, it's managed as any other file of the repository, and should be staged and committed when modified.

If you *really* don't want it to be committed, you can simply add the .gitignore name inside of the .gitignore file. Though, at that point, it makes more sense to just add all files you want to ignore to the .git/info/exclude list, which isn't staged and tracked already.

Since it's in the .git folder, it's not tracked like the files inside of the working directory are. Thus, you won't commit the exclude file and its contents.

The exclude file will affect only your local copy and the files you commit. So if you have some specific files others might not have, it makes sense to use the exclude file instead.

Say you're working with different IDEs and the IDE you're using makes files that some other developers might not have in their projects. Since .gitignore is meant to be present in all copies of the repository, assuming everyone will ignore the same files, you may commit the files specific to your environment by mistake.

If you add those files to the exclude file, you won't commit them, but also won't impose the action of ignoring those files onto other developers.

The syntax for the pattern matching in the exclude file are the exact same as the .gitignore file. For example, for Eclipse, you could add something along these lines to ignore many of the files generated by the IDE that you probably don't want to commit:

```
1   .project
2   .metadata
3   tmp/
4   tmp/**/*
5   *.tmp
6   *.bak
7   *.swp
8   local.properties
9   .classpath
10  .settings/
11  .loadpath
12  .factorypath
```

Here, we've decided to exclude/ignore the specific files called
.project and .metadata, as well as all files within the tmp
directory. Additionally, we've ignored all files that have the
.tmp, .bak and .swp extensions.

This same logic is applied to other files and directories.

5. Branches

First, what's a branch? As we said in the introduction, the idea behind branching is to manage multiple versions of a codebase, and that's what a branch is: *another version of that codebase.*

Similar to how commits are versions/snapshots of the codebase - each branch is a version of the codebase. However, each *branch* has a set of commits that lead to that state.

Let's say we're working with a fellow developer on a repository. For now, let's assume we're working on the same computer. They're fixing a very important bug, while we've been assigned the task of implementing a new feature.

We won't be ready for a while and can't take the chance of disturbing our colleague by committing some unfinished work. In the best-case scenario, we could accidentally change some behavior which breaks their code even more. In the worst-case scenario, since we don't usually package, test and refactor the code *while writing it for the first time*, we can break the entire project.

But still, we would like to commit our significant changes along the way and not wait for the bug to be fixed before recording our changes to the repository.

Initially, this seems like a counter-intuitive set of wishes. We don't want to disturb the existing repository, but we also want to commit changes to it along the way, other than just changes in the local repository.

This is the perfect opportunity to create a *branch*. We create a copy of the codebase, work on the feature as usual, commit changes, and push to the remote repository, on this new branch. Once we've finished the feature, and the colleague has fixed the bug, we can merge the work we did into a single, main branch.

Branching allows teams to work on different things in parallel, while also pushing changes to the remote branch, without negatively affecting other team members.

Conceptually, it would look something like this:

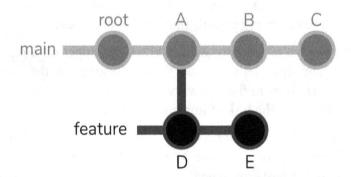

The master branch, which is the default name for the main branch, has its own set of commits that eventually lead up to the state it's currently in. The feature branch has its own history of commits, D, and E, and starts out by copying the state of the master branch at commit A. Commits D and E aren't present in the master branch, and represent fully new changes that are yet to be merged. This chapter covers both *merging* and *rebasing*.

So, our definition of a repository being a sequence of commits doesn't apply anymore. With the parallel tracks introduced by branches, a repository should rather be seen as a *graph* of commits. It's no longer one-dimensional.

Each *branch* is a sequence of commits, and each branch is a different version of the project. Each repository is a sequence of parallel *branches*.

Working on a Branch

Let's take a look at how we can work with branches, a key concept of Git repositories. Working with branches starts with creating one. This, as usual, is done with the git keyword, followed by the branch command and the name we'd like to apply to the branch:

```
1  $ git branch feature/addition
```

This one doesn't output anything, but, behind the scenes, it created our feature/addition branch. We can see all of our branches by solely running:

```
1  $ git branch
```

This outputs:

```
1    feature/addition
2  * master
```

That's our two existing branches, master and feature/addition. There is an asterisk in front of master, which means we are currently located on that branch. Creating a new one doesn't automatically switch us to it.

To switch to the new branch, we use another command, checkout, followed by the name of the branch:

```
1   $ git checkout feature/addition
```

That's it, we switched to the other branch:

```
1   Switched to branch 'feature/addition'
```

The git branch operation confirms it too:

```
1   * feature/addition
2     master
```

There we are. But wasn't it a bit tiring? Two commands to create and switch to a branch? We can easily combine commands, and tell Git to create a branch and switch us to it at the same time:

```
1   $ git checkout -b feature/soon-to-be-discarded
```

And now, we're switched directly to it:

```
1   Switched to a new branch 'feature/soon-to-be-discar\
2   ded'
```

Now, if we run:

```
1   $ git checkout
```

We're greeted with:

```
1    feature/addition
2  * feature/soon-to-be-discarded
3    master
```

Both git branch <branch-name> and git checkout -b <branch-name> will fail if given the name of an already existing branch:

```
1  $ git branch feature/addition
2  fatal: A branch named 'feature/addition' already ex\
3  ists.
```

Note: Just as you can checkout a branch, you can also checkout a commit, by providing the first 7 characters of the hash. This will effectively revert you back to that commit. We'll talk more about resetting and reverting in *Chapter 8 - Advanced Operations.*

Committing Changes to Different Branches

Let's get back to the feature/addition branch and do some work! We'll add an addition() method to our Calculator class:

```
1  public class Calculator {
2    public int addition(int a, int b) {
3      return a + b;
4    }
5  }
```

Then, let's add it and commit the change:

```
1  $ git add .
2  $ git commit -m "Adding a method to Calculator.java\
3   class"
```

Now, we've got a commit that's on our feature/addition branch, but not on master.

Let's run git log to see the commits made on each one:

```
1  $ git log
```

This results in:

```
1  commit 9078a515d0316673840b961d24d5626aa7139e8e
2  Author: francois <francois.dupire@nerthusconsulting\
3  .be>
4  Date:    Tue Jan 5 14:54:24 2021 +0100
5
6     Adding method to Calculator.java file
7
8  commit f9f47af8a0059a3b90dab8a6d0328fce910a0594
9  Author: francois <francois.dupire@nerthusconsulting\
10  .be>
11  Date:    Tue Jan 5 14:54:11 2021 +0100
12
```

```
13      Adding gitignore file
14
15   commit b174e76e34ba12e07e2333728c426f1c1afd8887
16   Author: francois <francois.dupire@nerthusconsulting\
17   .be>
18   Date:    Sun Jan 3 21:53:49 2021 +0100
19
20      Updated changelog with first log statement
21
22      ...
```

Then, let's switch back to master and view the log there:

```
1   $ git checkout master
2   $ git log
```

This results in:

```
1   commit f9f47af8a0059a3b90dab8a6d0328fce910a0594
2   Author: francois <francois.dupire@nerthusconsulting\
3   .be>
4   Date:    Tue Jan 5 14:54:11 2021 +0100
5
6      Adding gitignore file
7
8   commit b174e76e34ba12e07e2333728c426f1c1afd8887
9   Author: francois <francois.dupire@nerthusconsulting\
10  .be>
11  Date:    Sun Jan 3 21:53:49 2021 +0100
12
13      Updated changelog with first log statement
14
15      ...
```

We can see that the *same* commits can be seen for the "Updated changelog with first log statement" and "Added gitignore file" commits. They're shared between the branches, as feature/addition was copied from the master branch when these commits existed. It branched out from master, sharing these commits as the sequence of changes that made master the way it is.

However, feature/addition has an additional commit that isn't present in master, now.

When we checkout a branch, Git is changing the working tree so that it matches the commits made on that branch. As the master branch doesn't have the commit with the changes we added, the changes are missing. As soon as you checkout master, you'll even be able to see the file system updating before your eyes.

Gathering Branches Together

We've seen how to work on an alternate path of the repository. It's now time we learn how to gather work from two branches together. For example, we've made some changes in the feature/addition branch, and we'd like to merge it into master so that everyone can use the new functionality to work on their own tasks.

There are two operations to do that, merge and rebase, let's see what they both do.

Merge

We'll start with the merge of a branch into another. This can be done with the git merge command.

This command takes a branch name as an argument. This is the name of the branch we want to merge into the current one. So if we want to merge feature/addition into master, we'll move to master and merge feature/addition into it.

Fast-Forward Merge

Regarding the status of both branches, a merge can be applied using two different strategies - *fast-forward merge* and *non-fast-forward merge*.

Let's start off with the former, by navigating to the master branch and running:

```
1  $ git merge feature/addition
```

Then, we'll get this in the console:

```
1  Updating efb51ef..e700e3f
2  Fast-forward
3   Calculator.java | 6 +++++-
4   1 file changed, 5 insertions(+), 1 deletion(-)
```

As usual, Git shares some information of the operation's results with us.

On the second line, Git tells us it used the fast-forwarding strategy, meaning the only difference between the two branches are the commits on the branch we're merging (feature/addition) with. Thus, the HEAD reference, which points to the commit the working tree is representing, is simply updated to point to the last commit of feature/addition.

It doesn't actually need to *merge* files, since it can linearly just apply the commits from feature/addition that aren't present in master. We've seen that the log results are the same for both branches, except for the newest commit. In this case, merge would simply add that commit and new state to the master branch in a fast-forward merge operation.

On the first line, we get the commit hashes of current HEAD and new HEAD. Finally, the last lines are telling us what changes have been made to the working tree by applying this merge. In our case, we've got 5 insertions and one deletion. The deletion refers to the ending curly bracket, while the additions refer to the new lines we've put in the file.

The following two images illustrate what happened when we merged the feature/addition branch into the master branch. The next image show us the situation before the merge:

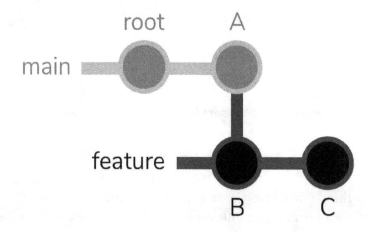

The feature branch is made from the A commit snapshot of master, and consists of A, B and C. B and C are new commits made to the feature branch, which aren't present in the master branch. The master branch consists only of A.

Since the `feature` branch just contains more commits on top of `master`, merging them means linearly applying these commits to `master`, after which, we've got:

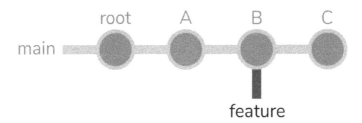

Both branches now contain the same commits in them. We can add new things to `feature` again, to make it diverge if we'd like to - the branch isn't deleted after merging. We just merge the commits.

Non-Fast-Forward Merge

What happens now if we've also got some commits on the master branch that are not on the other branch? This type of merge is also sometimes called the *true merge* since it actually merges, instead of concatenating new commits/states at the end.

Then, Git can't just update the HEAD pointer. Instead, it creates a merge commit that has two parents, both being last commits from both concerned branches.

Let's see that by running a quick example. First, let's say our colleague saw our implementation of the addition and decided to add another one to handle decimal numbers since we didn't cover that case:

```
1   public class Calculator {
2     public int addition(int a, int b) {
3       return a + b;
4     }
5
6     public double addition(double a, double b) {
7       return a + b;
8     }
9   }
```

This change is committed to master. Our colleague wasn't as considerate as we were, and didn't create a new branch to implement this change. In the meantime, on our side, we added some information about the brand new feature in the CHANGELOG.md file, but on our feature/addition branch:

```
1   $ git checkout feature/addition
2   $ echo "#2020-12-11" >> CHANGELOG.md
3   $ echo "* Added integer addition feature" >> CHANGE\
4   LOG.md"
```

Now, we've got a new change in the CHANGELOG.md file, and don't have the newest method of the Calculator.java class, which is on master.

We then finally go back to the master branch and merge:

```
1   $ git checkout master
2   $ git merge feature/addition
```

An editor should open asking us for a commit message for the merge commit, just like it popped up when we didn't supply a commit message:

```
1  Merge branch 'feature/addition'
2  ## Please enter a commit message to explain why thi\
3  s merge is necessary,
4  ## especially if it merges an updated upstream into\
5   a topic branch.
6  ##
7  ## Lines starting with '#' will be ignored, and an \
8  empty message aborts
9  ## the commit.
```

We can go with the default message for the sake of the example, but in real-life situations, a few more words might makes things clearer as to what and why we're merging. This will be greatly appreciated by all team members, as they'll be aware of what's going on on the joint codebase.

After saving the message, the following is shown in the console:

```
1  Merge made by the 'recursive' strategy.
2   CHANGELOG.md | 2 ++
3   1 file changed, 2 insertions(+)
```

When fast-forward is not an option, recursive is the default merge strategy. As said earlier, it'll create a commit whose both parents are the last commits from the two merged branches.

As shown by the following schema, the resulting situation is a bit different than with a fast-forward merge:

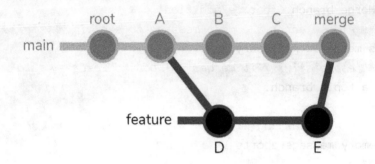

Conflicts

There is a last situation we should talk about. It's an important one as this happens a lot when working with other people on the same project: **conflicts**.

A conflict occurs when two people modified the same parts of the same file. Let's see that by going back to our feature/addition branch, and implement the decimal addition as well (let's say we didn't see our colleague has already done it), but let's introduce a tiny difference:

```
1   $ git checkout feature/addition
```

And modify the Calculator.java file:

```
1   public double addition(double a, double b) {
2       return b + a;
3   }
```

We inverted the operands in the return statement, so that our modifications are not exactly the same as our colleague's, but still produce the same results. Let's save and commit this change:

```
1  $ git add Calculator.java
2  $ git commit -m "Added addition method for doubles"
```

We then go back on the master branch and merge again:

```
1  $ git checkout master
2  $ git merge feature/addition
```

We should get the following output:

```
1  Auto-merging Calculator.java
2  CONFLICT (content): Merge conflict in Calculator.ja\
3  va
4  Automatic merge failed; fix conflicts and then comm\
5  it the result.
```

And here is what our Calculator.java file looks like now, after trying to merge:

```
1  public class Calculator {
2    public int addition(int a, int b) {
3      return a + b;
4    }
5
6    public double addition(double a, double b) {
7  <<<<<<< HEAD
8      return a + b;
9  =======
10     return b + a;
11 >>>>>>> feature/addition
12   }
13 }
```

Again, Git is giving us some intel we can use to decide what to do. The <<<<<<< part tells us a difference causing a conflict is starting right here.

Just after that we got the name of the current reference (HEAD, so the last commit of master here). Then, we got the changes brought on that branch.

Right after, there is a line drawn with minus signs (=======). This means we're stepping into the changes of the other branch, that come after that line. Finally, we've got the arrow symbols, >>>>>>>, followed by the name of the branch we're merging, meaning that difference stops here.

In this case, it's telling us that HEAD/master has return a + b in this line, while feature/addition has return b + a in this line.

To solve the conflict, we've got to decide what goes into our resulting file:

- The line from master?
- The line from feature/addition?
- Both lines?
- None?

That's up to us, and all we've got to do is update the file so that it doesn't contain any line from the merge anymore (<<<<<<<, >>>>>>> and =======), and contains the content we want it to contain.

git merge –continue

Here, let's say we want to keep the line from master, then we must update our file so that it looks like this:

```
1  public class Calculator {
2    public int addition(int a, int b) {
3      return a + b;
4    }
5
6    public double addition(double a, double b) {
7      return a + b;
8    }
9  }
```

Once saved, we must add the file to the index again. Then, we'll run the `git merge --continue` command, telling Git we're done with resolving the conflicts and that we'd like to continue merging:

```
1  $ git add Calculator.java
2  $ git merge --continue
```

After that, Git will asks us for a merge commit message, as it did earlier. We set what we want, save, and we're done!

Traditionally, you'd add the file again and perform a `commit`, adding a message about the merge conflict solution. However, since Git 2.12, the `git merge --continue` command essentially finishes the commit for us, asking us for a message for that commit. We've essentially fixed the conflict ourselves, by updating the file, and then committed it to master using `git merge --continue`.

Resolving conflicts like this can become quite cumbersome when there are a lot of them. Graphical merge tools exist to help us achieve this. Learning them is not in the scope of this book, but be aware that they exist.

git merge –abort

Alternatively, instead of continuing, we can use `git merge --abort` to abort the entire merge. This can be done if you ran into a huge issue with the merge, or if a lot of code needs to be changed. In that case, it might very well be easier to just abort the merge, fix the code in your IDE and then merge again.

Let's re-introduce an issue to the `feature/addition`'s `Calculator.java` class:

```
1    $ git checkout feature/addition
```

And change the class:

```
1    public class Calculator {
2      public int addition(int a, int b) {
3        return a + b;
4      }
5
6      public double addition(double a, double b) {
7        // Causes merge conflict
8        return b + a;
9      }
10   }
```

Note that the code in this branch is the same one we had before the merge. The code we manually fixed while merging into master stays on master. If we tried doing another merge between these two without changing anything, the conflict is already known to Git and automatically resolved by taking the code we've manually fixed.

Now, we've put in a new comment, that causes a merge conflict. Let's try merging again:

```
1  $ git checkout master
2  $ git merge feature/addition
3  Auto-merging Calculator.java
4  CONFLICT (content): Merge conflict in Calculator.ja\
5  va
6  Automatic merge failed; fix conflicts and then comm\
7  it the result.
```

Our `Calculator.java` class now again contains content that shows us where the merge conflict occurred:

```
1  public class Calculator {
2    public int addition(int a, int b) {
3      return a + b;
4    }
5
6    public double addition(double a, double b) {
7  <<<<<<< HEAD
8      return a + b;
9  =======
10     // Causes merge conflict
11     return b + a;
12 >>>>>>> feature/addition
13   }
14 }
```

Now, instead of fixing the conflict, let's just abort the `merge`:

```
1  $ git merge --abort
```

Now, if we open the `Calculator.java` file, the conflict is there no more:

```
1  public class Calculator {
2    public int addition(int a, int b) {
3      return a + b;
4    }
5
6    public double addition(double a, double b) {
7      return a + b;
8    }
9  }
```

Rebase

As mentioned earlier, merging is one way to bring the content of two branches together, but there is another one: *rebasing*.

Conceptually, rebasing a branch onto another is telling Git that we want out commits to be reapplied on top of that other branch's commits.

Let's illustrate this by creating another branch for the subtraction feature, and then adding the implementation of that feature. While our fellow developer is creating an Application class to call our Calculator project.

Let's make the branch:

```
1  $ git checkout -b feature/subtraction
```

And on that branch, let's add the subtraction functionality:

```
1   public class Calculator {
2     // Other methods are hidden for brevity
3
4     public int subtraction(int a, int b) {
5       return a - b;
6     }
7
8     public double subtraction(double a, double b) {
9       return a - b;
10    }
11  }
```

Then, let's add and commit this file:

```
1   $ git add Calculator.java
2   $ git commit -m "Added subtraction method"
```

Let's see what our last commit hash is by running git log
-1:

```
1   commit 4076a7b2917b346a029f9cceaced85e61403695d (HE\
2   AD -> feature/subtraction)
3   Author: francois <francois.dupire@nerthusconsulting\
4   .be>
5   Date:   Fri Dec 11 07:54:01 2020 +0100
6
7       Added subtraction feature
```

We talked about the git log command in the previous chapter.
Notice the usage of the -1 option. It allows to reduce the
printed commits to the last one. Let's keep this commit hash
in mind.

As a matter of fact, we can see this option as -x where x is a number. Therefore, we can use git log -10 to print the last 10 commits of the branch!

And now, let's go back to master and make an Application.java file that will host some logic that uses the Calculator class:

```
1   $ git checkout master
2   $ touch Application.java
```

And now, within that file, we'll add something along the lines of:

```
1   public class Application {
2     public static void main(String[] args) {
3       Calculator calculator = new Calculator();
4       System.out.println(calculator.addition(1, 2)); \
5   // Should be 3
6       System.out.println(calculator.addition(1.5, 3.2\
7   )); // Should be 4.7
8     }
9   }
```

Of course, let's add and commit this change:

```
1   $ git add Application.java
2   $ git commit -m "Added Application to call the Calc\
3   ulator"
```

Now, it's time to *rebase*. This time, instead of going to the branch that we'd want to change (merge into) like last time, we go to the branch with the changes and *rebase* it to the branch we'd like to update the code in.

In our case, we'll call git rebase master while on the feature/subtraction branch:

```
1  $ git checkout feature/subtraction
2  $ git rebase master
```

Now, this results in:

```
1  First, rewinding head to replay your work on top of\
2   it...
3  Applying: Added subtraction feature
```

So, Git says it's rewinding HEAD, meaning it puts the HEAD pointer on the last commit of master. Then, it applies our latest commit from feature/subtraction onto that HEAD. We've *stacked* the commit from feature/subtraction onto master.

Let's run the log command again:

```
1  commit f3bdaa8309babb79326dde4007f93dbfb91bb191 (HE\
2  AD -> feature/subtraction)
3  Author: francois <francois.dupire@nerthusconsulting\
4  .be>
5  Date:   Fri Dec 11 07:54:01 2020 +0100
6
7      Added subtraction feature
```

There, our commit hash has changed! The reason is this isn't the same commit anymore, it is a new commit with the same content as the previous one, but with another parent.

Let's have a look at the previous commit as well by running git log -2:

```
 1   commit f3bdaa8309babb79326dde4007f93dbfb91bb191 (HE\
 2   AD -> feature/subtraction)
 3   Author: francois <francois.dupire@nerthusconsulting\
 4   .be>
 5   Date:   Fri Dec 11 07:54:01 2020 +0100
 6
 7       Added subtraction feature
 8
 9   commit c776831d3eb07fb5da65d6bd729b787c5aea16d6 (ma\
10   ster)
11   Author: francois <francois.dupire@nerthusconsulting\
12   .be>
13   Date:   Fri Dec 11 07:59:15 2020 +0100
14
15       Added Application to call the Calculator
```

This is our last commit from master. So, the feature/subtraction branch now starts from the last commit of master rather than the one before that, as it used to when we made the branch itself.

Again, it's easier to digest this through an image, so here an illustration of the rebase operation's result:

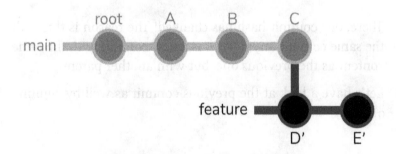

Conflict Resolution

And what happens if we have conflicting changes? The conflict resolution isn't that different than with a merge, except we don't have a merge commit with conflict resolution.

Instead, Git will stop for each conflicting commit and ask us to resolve them directly. The changes will be embedded in the new version of that commit.

Once a conflict is solved, we run `git rebase --continue` (instead of `git merge --continue` in a merge). Or, we can run `git rebase --abort` if we'd like to abort the rebase.

Additionally, if you don't want to abort the entire rebase, but can't deal with a specific conflict, you can use `git rebase --skip`.

Deleting a Branch

Finally, we may want to discard a branch we created because it lead us nowhere, or because we merged it successfully and simply don't need it anymore.

In order to do that, we must be on another branch than the one we're deleting. Any branch is fine, as long as we're not on the sinking ship. Then, we just run the command `git branch -d <branch_name>`.

Let's do that with our branch `feature/soon-to-be-discarded` and `feature/addition` that we merged earlier, since we don't need it anymore:

```
1  $ git branch -d feature/soon-to-be-discarded
2  $ git branch -d feature/addition
```

The result is quite simple, Git let us know it deleted the
requested branch:

```
1  Deleted branch feature/soon-to-be-discarded (was b1\
2  74e76)
3  Deleted branch feature/addition (was 0e5cddc).
```

In addition to that, it tells us which was the last commit of
that branch. What happens if we decide to delete a branch we
didn't merge yet?

Let's say we're not satisfied with what we did for the subtraction feature and want to delete the branch. Then Git won't
allow the operation to be done, saying there are commits that
are yet to be merged from that branch into the current one:

```
1  error: The branch 'feature/subtraction' is not full\
2  y merged.
3  If you are sure you want to delete it, run 'git bra\
4  nch -D feature/subtraction'.
```

But, there is a way out if we still want to delete the branch
without merging it - using the -D flag instead:

```
1  $ git branch -D feature/subtraction
```

And then, the branch is no more and the unique commits on
it are definitely lost:

```
1   Deleted branch feature/subtraction (was f3bdaa8).
```

Renaming a Branch

Renaming a branch can be done easily, using the -m flag alongside the git branch command. Let's make a new branch:

```
1   $ git checkout -b newbrancg
2   Switched to a new branch 'newbrancg'
```

Oops. It should've been newbranch. We were quick to use the shorthand form of creating and moving into a branch, but at the cost of making a typo in the name. No need to delete it and make a new one, we can simply rename it.

To rename a branch, you'll want to be checked out on the branch you want to rename, and then run:

```
1   $ git branch -m newbranch
```

Running either of these two won't show any output, but let's check if the name has been changed by running git branch:

```
1   $ git branch
2   master
3   * newbranch
```

Looks good!

Now, let's make another branch:

```
1  $ git branch anotherbranch
```

And while still being on newbranch, let's try to rename it to
an already taken name - anotherbranch:

```
1  $ git branch -m anotherbranch
2  fatal: A branch named 'anotherbranch' already exist\
3  s.
```

If you'd like to force the renaming of the current branch, you
can use -M:

```
1  $ git branch -M anotherbranch
```

Now, when we check what branches are active:

```
1  $ git branch
2  * anotherbranch
3  master
```

> **Note:** This will override anotherbranch with the
> contents of newbranch. If you force Git to rename
> the branch into an existing name, the original name
> holder will be overridden. Avoid using -M if you're
> not sure that you want to drop a branch while
> renaming an old one.

6. Remote Repositories

At this stage of the book, we've built a solid understanding of how to manage a local Git repository - how to create one for a project, how the working directory and staging area work, how to add and remove branches, switch between them, commit changes, as well as merge and rebase the work we've done so far.

We're equipped with the knowledge that allows us to follow multiple parallel tracks of work, but also cooperate more easily with our colleagues. However, one thing that *wasn't* so convenient is that all the work so far has been done on the same machine. Let's face it, that's not very realistic.

Sure, we've had branches to separate workflows, and we've simulated our colleagues working on different tasks by switching between branches and committing code changes, but it was all done on the same machine.

Now is the time to evolve towards working with remote repositories, so that each collaborator can use their own machine, at a different place, at any given time. This will be the focus of this chapter.

Through this chapter, we'll learn what a remote repository is and how we can work with them. We'll then take a look at how to set one up for free using GitHub, and after that, we'll take a look at how we can set up a link between a local and a remote repository.

Then, we'll go over tracking branches and the way Git handles remote repositories. Finally, we'll see the different operations Git offers to sync both kinds of repositories together.

What is a Remote Repository?

Let's remember what we talked about in *Chapter 2 - Source Code Management*. Git is a distributed VCS, meaning each person working on a repository gets their own copy of the code history. A remote repository is nothing more than a copy of the repository we're working on, located elsewhere. We'll send and receive updates to and from such repositories.

You usually start out with a *local repository*, like we did for our Calculator. Then, you'll likely host it somewhere public (with or without access identification), and then have other people clone it. Once cloned, they all have their own *local version* of your *remote repository*. Similar to how we've worked on our own local repository so far, you'll be working with much the same approach, because most of the work you'll be doing is local.

Once you're finished with the local changes, you can *push* your own changes to the remote repository, and *pull* the changes made by others, into your local repository.

Usually, a centralized remote repository acts as a hub for all the contributors of a project. This doesn't mean Git is a centralized VCS. The centralized remote repository is just a handy way to collaborate on a project, since again, most of the work you'll be doing will be *local* and decentralized.

Setting up a Remote Repository

Let's get more practical and set up a remote repository. An easy way to do that is to create one on [GitHub][www.github.com], the most well-known and used platform for hosting Git repositories.

GitHub is owned by Microsoft, which acquired it back in 2018. It's worth noting that GitHub is just a tool/platform built around the Git tool. It's by no means an official hosting service related to Git, just the most popular one.

Other repository hosting services include GitLab[15] and Bit-Bucket[16].

Even though these services are not officially a part of Git, they're so deeply entrenched and commonly used together that they might as well be.

If you're just looking to perform Version Control on a project you're working on yourself - there's no real need to set up a remote repository. Remote repositories are meant for ease of sharing and collaboration with other people - be it colleagues that work in the same office with you, or people from the other side of the planet.

Create a GitHub Account

For starters, let's create an account on GitHub:

---

[15]https://about.gitlab.com/
[16]https://bitbucket.org/product

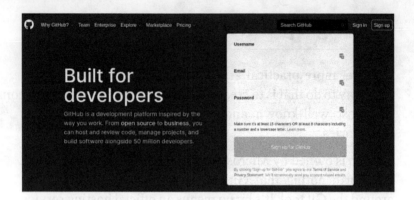

Once we've achieved that, we can launch the creation of new repository, using the left panel New button:

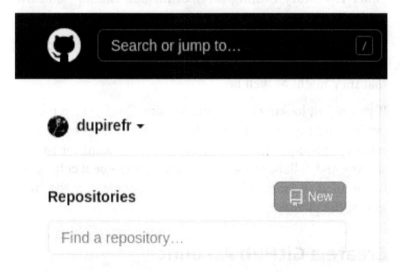

We'll be presented a web form. You can choose to make the repository *Public* or *Private*. If it's public, anyone will be able to view the source code, but not everyone will be able to commit changes to it. This is great for open-source projects, tools, or simply sharing data and information with people.

A *Private* repository will be invisible to everyone except for the people you allow by inviting them via email. Of course, they'll need to have GitHub accounts to be able to view it. Other than that, you can have GitHub create a README.md, .gitignore and license file. If you're creating a remote repository *before* creating a local project, you can select these options, and then *pull* them from the remote repository to your *local* repository on your machine.

Then, you can work locally again. Since we've already got these files, we'll skip these options.

Finally, we need to come up with a name for our repository - calculator seems fitting. You can optionally also put in a description if you'd like:

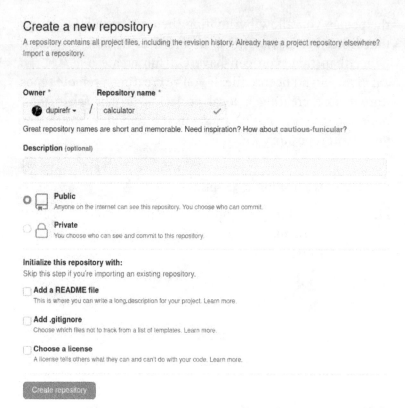

Then, we'll be taken to a page that explains what we can do to start using our newly created remote repository. As we already mentioned - since we have the code and repository from the previous chapters, we'll go with the second option - *"Push an existing repository from the command line"*:

If we had created this remote repository *before* creating a local one, we'd now *clone* this repository, creating a local one on our machine, or since it's still empty - we could create an empty repository locally and add this one as the remote.

GitHub even lays this process out for us in the first option, and inputs the values we'll want to use as well:

```
1  $ echo "# calculator" >> README.md
2  $ git init
3  $ git add README.md
4  $ git commit -m "first commit"
5  $ git branch -M main
6  $ git remote add origin https://github.com/dupirefr\
7  /calculator.git
8  $ git push -u origin main
```

We're familiar with all the commands up until the git remote add origin command, and the git push command. We'll cover those in this chapter.

It's worth noting that GitHub tells us to rename the current branch to `main`, via the `git branch -M main` statement. The current branch is the default one, created by Git, when we run `git init`. The default Git branch name Git uses is `master`. Effectively, this line renames our `master` branch into `main`.

Since October 1st of 2020, GitHub renamed[17] the default branch, alongside other organizations[18] in the Git ecosystem, from `master` to `main` to avoid negative connotations of the word. It's also announced that Git will change the default branch name in the future[19], though, as of writing this book, it's still in the transition phase. During the setup phase, you might be prompted to choose the default name Git uses when repositories are initialized. If not, you can easily rename the branch after creating a repository just like GitHub instructs us to.

Until Git officially implements this change, we'll stick to the up-to-date version in this book, renaming the branch manually.

This page will be the default page of our repository, and is currently located under: www.github.com/dupirefr/calculator.

Chose a Communication Protocol

Before going into the commands above and using them, let's first finish up the setup phase and choose a communication protocol.

Dealing with remote repositories can be done using several communication protocols. Among them are HTTP(s) and SSH, those two being the most used.

---

[17]https://github.com/github/renaming
[18]https://lore.kernel.org/git/pull.656.v4.git.1593009996.gitgitgadget@gmail.com/
[19]https://sfconservancy.org/news/2020/jun/23/gitbranchname/

HTTP(s)

Should we use the first option, our credentials would be prompted at least for the first attempt to send or receive data to or from the remote repository. At that moment, our operating system might offer us to store those credentials in a manager in order to avoid asking us again in the future.

Remember, though, that if the protocol is HTTP and not HTTPs - those credentials are not encrypted before being sent to the server. Fortunately for us, GitHub uses HTTPs, but that might not be the case of another server (one set up by a company, for example).

SSH

On the other hand, if we chose to use the second option, SSH, then we're certain to be safe. Like HTTPs, SSH is using asymmetric encryption to exchange data with other network entities. It requires the server to be configured to use it, though.

First, we need to generate a pair of private/public key, which can be done with the command:

```
1  $ ssh-keygen -t rsa -b 4096 -C "francois.dupire@ner\
2  thusconsulting.be"
```

This means we want to create a key using the RSA encryption algorithm (-t option) with keys made of 4096 bits (-b) and our email address as a comment (-C) for the key file. It doesn't have to be the same as our GitHub's account, but that can be a handy way to remember this key is linked to the email address of our GitHub account. We also could have named it

'*GitHub*' and have separate keys for each service that requires it.

We'll be prompted a few questions - the location of the saved file, the passphrase for it, and retyping the same passphrase. These can all be answered by pressing Enter, meaning we are choosing the default values.

The default value for the passphrase is that it doesn't exist, meaning the private key won't be encrypted. If we'd like to, we can set up a passphrase, which will be required when we use the key. Our operating system credentials manager can be of some help to avoid retyping the passphrase each time.

At this point, the key pair should've been generated under the directory .ssh of our home directory on MacOS and Linux and C:\Users\User/.ssh/ for Windows. Two files should be found there: id_rsa and id_rsa.pub. The former contains the private key, while the latter contains the public one.

Now, the SSH agent must be up and running and now about our key. A simple shh-agent command should tell us if the agent is running. If it's not, you'll want to boot it up via:

```
1   $ eval `ssh-agent`
```

Or, on Windows:

```
1   $ start-ssh-agent
```

If it is, then we've got to add our key to the agent:

```
1   $ ssh-add ~/id_rsa
```

Or, on Windows:

```
1  $ ssh-add C:\Users\User/.shh/id_rsa
```

As the agent reads keys from the ~/.ssh directory by default, our key will get picked up at startup.

If our agent wasn't started, then it probably means it doesn't start automatically. If that were the case, we could set up our operating system to automatically run the agent at startup.

Now, we're all set up locally. The final step we've got to do here is adding the public key to GitHub. This way, it'll be able to use it to encrypt data it needs to send us.

To do that, let's go to the SSH and GPG keys settings section, and click the New SSH key button:

We'll be taken to a form where we've to give the key a title and paste the content of the ~/.ssh/id_rsa.pub file:

SSH keys / Add new

Title

My SSH Key

Key

```
ssh-rsa
AAAAB3NzaC1yc2EAAAADAQABAAACAQDd6gafwDyjflpEpdF8gEGGeDJbHmj6skwac8XL7W9BslOLwEH3lsBN
T6M9984VYRpPfRinpcKOJMmLsxlzG1wD1fvwNkS6Qfv963S6gsPLsl/l0CON6VuO4pV2cx3aztrxKES59HpLAnu9
LFFbyOuL7jAxs0KqdKuYqwvAGv6ykeRYFTKpKUZ3eff1wMUOGldNN2jSNoWbc9C6N516/lJY/vEEg+
/HgvMhhVqTR48XpdJGQX+Vk8xl2xeTmbMmeQx7ks5xgWz1rnvRURbJGc8+ro9DF+hcUcAJyjMsJfgB1KUV2rAD
o6oXVPoiBrv4+XSUsCU
/ExQA954dPmfrVwxJml5qoY9BpjTzCltFd+4Ry+kKvSoaOyHn4K9x0qxHJr5qkxnbf63VnPy7pfoFsAB7WyxOkJBpw
m7gplwghlyGB/5wQZ9+Puijz S1jjN/pleSF7I+ZWlcvUtgkXx0
/4/4nUUtmOGFu4UgYcnW88RF27bh7etMGeWFXpetLiizLNvVxvdGCB9u2TF/rPtycTiizJJjFzV6nfAsHBErek0a
/lN2wrllUvFlW4rUOOX0igmEMUT0UZH95gpp5Lcm754osv
/ouU8bXDzUTBHcLT+ty6ggcDWUMXAosjfSWDV0IRM4NnN8ChCLZAvYGxWDkl529d8t
/Gnb7SFNzdu9rhMgQwQ== dupire.francois@gmail.com
```

Add SSH key

Finally, we can click the Add SSH key button, and we're good
to go!

Pushing Our First Commit to the Remote Repository

Now, with all the configuration done, we can go back to our local repository and tie it with the remote repository we've created. It's hosted under www.github.com/dupirefr/calculator[20],
and we'd use this URL if we were to use HTTPs. Since
we're using SSH, this repository can be accessed through
git@github.com:dupirefr/calculator.git.

Let's add the remote repository, rename the branch and *push*
the change to the main branch:

---

[20]www.github.com/dupirefr/calculator

```
1  $ git remote add origin git@github.com:dupirefr/cal\
2  culator.git
3  $ git branch -M main
4  $ git push -u origin main
```

The git remote command essentially just changes our local config file. Here, we've added a remote repository. We've decided to use the reference name origin for it, since it'll be the origin of our code. This name is simply the convention used by the vast majority of developers, and also the default name for your remote repository. You can put anything other than origin as well, if you'd like. Then, we've supplied the URL of the remote repository to be tied with origin.

In the future, instead of typing the entire URL to the repository, we can simply use origin. You can, by all means use the URL as well - most people simply find it way more convenient to use a short name to definitively reference a remote repository's location, for that project.

The command can be summarized as:

```
1  $ git remote add <reference_name_for_repo> <URL/loc\
2  ation_of_repo>
```

Where the remote add command just adds this set of values to our config file.

After setting it like this, whenever we wish to perform any actions with the remote repository, we'll reference origin instead of the entire URL since it's far more convenient that way. Git will know which repository we're referring to since it's all set in the config file due to the git remote add command.

Then, we rename the `master` branch to `main` and `push` the changes to `origin main`. In other words, we push to the `main` branch of `origin`, which is `git@github.com:dupirefr/calculator.git`. We'll talk about the -u flag a bit later.

This command can be generalized to:

```
1  $ git push <location_of_repo> <branch_of_that_repo>
```

Running this set of commands results in something along the lines of:

```
1   Counting objects: 40, done.
2   Delta compression using up to 4 threads.
3   Compressing objects: 100% (17/17), done.
4   Writing objects: 100% (37/37), 301 bytes | 0 bytes/\
5   s, done.
6   Total 3 (delta 1), reused 0 (delta 0)
7   remote: Resolving deltas: 100% (1/1), completed wit\
8   h 1 local object.
9   To https://github.com/dupirefr/calculator
10     06c148c..7f4abbb  main -> main
11  Branch main set up to track remote branch main from\
12   origin.
```

Now, if we have a look at the repository on GitHub we'll see that our local changes are there:

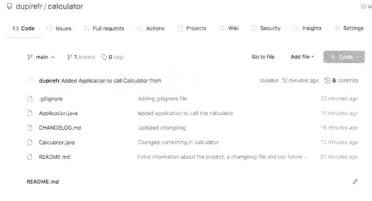

Calculator Project

By default, GitHub takes the contents of the README file and renders it on the front page. This is typically the place where you describe your project and include setup information, for example. Keep this in mind when writing it.

For the purpose of this chapter, we'll also impersonate a fellow collaborator of ours joining our great project. Now that we've created a remote repository they can access, let's see how they can make a local copy of our repository, make changes to it, and push them back to the remote repository from where we can pull again.

As the remote repository exists and has commits on it, they must *clone* it. Git has a dedicated command to copy a remote repository to a machine - `git clone`. This commands takes the repository link as well as an optional directory name if we don't want the repository to be cloned in a directory of the same name.

They can also *clone* a repository using GitHub's GUI, though, we'll focus on Git itself. Let's clone the project under a directory named `calculator-collaborator`.

First, we'll want to move out of the project directory we're in, into a free space where we'd like to make our new directory. We'll make it next to our project's directory for the sake of simplicity:

```
1  # Move out of the directory of our project
2  # to simulate a collaborator running this command
3  # on a different machine
4  $ cd ..
5  # git clone URL <optional_name>
6  $ git clone git@github.com:dupirefr/calculator.git \
7  calculator-collaborator
```

We could've skipped the name fully, in which case, it'd just use the same name as the remote repository. In this case, it'd be calculator. We've supplied a name to differentiate between these projects on our machine.

This command will output something along the lines of:

```
1  Cloning into 'calculator-collaborator'...
2  remote: Enumerating objects: 37, done.
3  remote: Counting objects: 100% (37/37), done.
4  remote: Compressing objects: 100% (17/17), done.
5  remote: Total 37 (delta 13), reused 36 (delta 12), \
6  pack-reused 0
7  Receiving objects: 100% (37/37), done.
8  Resolving deltas: 100% (13/13), done.
```

And now we've two copies of the repository on our machine. We'll use both in this chapter to see the interactions between collaborators working on the same project.

For clarity, let's at least update the username associated to the new local repository. In the new directory, called `calculator-collaborator`, let's change the local configuration:

```
1  $ git config user.name collaborator
```

This updates the local configuration file, as we haven't used the `--global` flag and sets the name of the user for that specific repository to `collaborator`.

Tracking Branches

Now, before digging into the remote operations, let's talk a bit about how Git handles working with remote repositories.

First, let's run the following command in our Git repository:

```
1  $ git branch -a
```

The `-a` flag shows both the local and remote branches. This will print the following:

```
1  * main
2    remotes/origin/main
```

`-a` is the short option for `--all`, meaning we are listing all the branches in our repository. Thus, we've got our `main` branch (we renamed that a few steps ago), and a branch we didn't create: `remotes/origin/main`. What's that branch then?

It's the local copy of the `main` branch of the `origin` repository. Such branches are called *tracking branches*. Its real name is `origin/main`, Git is prefixing it with `remotes/` so that we can distinguish those from the other local branches.

But, we can't stress that enough: *those branches are also local*! They are merely copies of what was on the remote branch at the time of the last update we performed. If somebody updates the remote repository main branch, the `origin/main` branch won't be updated without further action on our side.

The purpose of that branch, then, is to gather, on demand, the history modifications from the remote repository. After that, we can update our own branches with the changes made on that remote repository branch.

When we update some of the files in the working directory, they're compared against the local version of the remote repository. That's how Git tracks if we're ahead of the remote or not, at least compared to when we last updated our local copy.

We'll dedicate the next section to learn how to interact with remote repositories, and concretely how those tracking branches come into play.

Sending and Retrieving Remote Modifications

Now, we're going to see how to send our local commits to a remote repository, as well as get commits from that remote repository and integrate them locally.

The push Command

Let's begin with the sending part, called pushing. We've already seen the push command in action earlier, but let's get into more details here.

The push commands sends a given branch's commits to a given remote repository branch. Let's have a look at the command we ran before:

```
1   $ git push -u origin main
```

Here, we've sent our local main branch's commits to the origin remote repository. By default, it'll go on a branch of the same name on that repository. You don't have to be checked out on your local main for the contents of that branch to be pushed to origin's main when you run this command.

Also, the main in this command isn't the destination. It's the branch you want to push. This command can be generalized to:

```
1   $ git push <remote_repo_location> <which_branch_to_\
2   send>
```

We can also notice the -u option. This is actually just the short version for --set-upstream. This means that, from that moment on, the main branch of the origin remote will be the default branch we're pushing the current local branch to.

So, if we're on our local main and just pushed to the origin's main with the -u flag - next time we run the command, we can simply write:

```
1   $ git push
```

If we specify neither the destination, nor the local branch
we're pushing, it'll use the latest configuration set by -u. The
upstream link between our main and the remote's main is set,
and is now the default push. Of course, we can regularly push
without this flag, if we'd like - it's just a convenience flag that
allows us to skip retyping common commands.

Let's add information about the remote repository in the
README file:

```
1   $ echo "## Remote repository" >> README.md
2   $ echo "The remote repository for this project is h\
3   osted on GitHub at the following address: https://g\
4   ithub.com/dupirefr/calculator" >> README.md
5   $ git commit -am "Added explanation about the remot\
6   e repository"
7   $ git push
```

That operation prints works just as it worked before we used
the -u flag:

```
1    Enumerating objects: 5, done.
2    Counting objects: 100% (5/5), done.
3    Delta compression using up to 8 threads
4    Compressing objects: 100% (3/3), done.
5    Writing objects: 100% (3/3), 439 bytes | 439.00 KiB\
6    /s, done.
7    Total 3 (delta 1), reused 0 (delta 0)
8    remote: Resolving deltas: 100% (1/1), completed wit\
9    h 1 local object.
10   To github.com:dupirefr/calculator.git
11      c776831..3649cab  main -> main
```

When we push changes to the remote branch, the changes are also saved in the origin/main branch (which is, remember, local) to reflect the changes in the actual remote branch.

Pushing to Branches Explicitly

So far, we've let Git auto-select the branch we're pushing to. If we push our local main, it'll push to to the remote main. If we push a branch that exists locally, but not remotely, it'll just create that remote branch and push to it.

If you'd like to specify both the branch you're pushing, and the one you're pushing to, you can use the explicit version of the push command:

```
$ git push origin main:another_branch
```

Here, we must specify the name of the branch to push (local) and the name of the receiving branch (remote).

Finally, what happens if someone else has pushed commits on the remote repository, and we want to push ours as well? Let's impersonate our colleague and create a new multiply() method in our Calculator class:

```
1  public class Calculator {
2    // Other methods ommitted for brevity
3
4    public int multiply(int a, int b) {
5      return a * b;
6    }
7
8    public double mutiply(double a, double b) {
9      return a * b;
10   }
11 }
```

Let's commit and push:

```
1  git commit -am "Added a feature to multiply integer\
2   and decimal numbers"
3  git push
```

Now, let's come back to our own copy of the project and try to push a commit with a COLLABORATORS.md file:

```
1  # Exit collaborator's directory
2  $ cd..
3  # Enter our own directory
4  $ cd calculator
5  $ echo "# Collaborators" >> COLLABORATORS.md
6  $ echo "* francois" >> COLLABORATORS.md
7  $ echo "* collaborator" >> COLLABORATORS.md
8  $ git add COLLABORATORS.md
9  $ git commit -m "Added information about the projec\
10 t collaborators"
11 $ git push
```

We'll see that our push is simply rejected:

```
1   ! [rejected]          main -> main (fetch first)
2   error: failed to push some refs to 'git@github.com:\
3   dupirefr/calculator.git'
4   hint: Updates were rejected because the remote cont\
5   ains work that you do
6   hint: not have locally. This is usually caused by a\
7   nother repository pushing
8   hint: to the same ref. You may want to first integr\
9   ate the remote changes
10  hint: (e.g., 'git pull ...') before pushing again.
11  hint: See the 'Note about fast-forwards' in 'git pu\
12  sh --help' for details.
```

Here, Git is telling us that the remote contains commits we don't have, and advises us to integrate those changes locally before pushing. We can't push if we're outdated. We first have to update ourselves, before trying to add new features or commit changes.

The fetch Command

Now that we've covered pushing commits to a remote repository, let's see how to get commits from it.

As we've seen in the end of the last section, we're out of sync with the remote repository's main branch. Our colleague has pushed a commit that we must integrate before going further and push our own changes.

Well, to sync up our local branch, we can begin by using the fetch command. This will update the origin/main branch of our local repository:

```
1  $ git fetch origin main
```

Again, this doesn't update the local main branch, nor the remote main branch. This updates the local copy of the remote's main branch, that exists so we can compare it to our own local one. The call can be generalized to:

```
1  $ git fetch <remote_repository> <remote_branch>
```

That, again, produces its share of logs:

```
1  remote: Enumerating objects: 5, done.
2  remote: Counting objects: 100% (5/5), done.
3  remote: Compressing objects: 100% (2/2), done.
4  remote: Total 3 (delta 1), reused 3 (delta 1), pack\
5  -reused 0
6  Unpacking objects: 100% (3/3), 390 bytes | 195.00 K\
7  iB/s, done.
8  From github.com:dupirefr/calculator
9   * branch            main        -> FETCH_HEAD
10    3649cab..ba2c556  main        -> origin/main
```

The third line, starting from the end, tells us from which repository we're getting the commits from. The next one explains that the remote main branch data have been written to a specific Git reference, FETCH_HEAD. This reference contains the last fetched data, similar to how HEAD contains the last committed data. Finally, the last line tells us which range of commits have been added to origin/main.

Our origin/main branch is up-to-date then! But, we're working on the main branch, not the origin/main branch. Here, we've got the latest state on one branch, and we haven't messed up our own main branch before we can review what's going on if we'd like.

To update our own local main branch, all we've to do is to either merge the origin/main branch into our main branch, or rebase the main branch on top of the origin/main.

Let's go for a merge here:

```
1  # Make sure you're on main
2  $ git checkout main
3  $ git merge origin/main
```

We'll be prompted with the same kind of logs we've already seen before:

```
1  Merge made by the 'recursive' strategy.
2   Calculator.java | 8 ++++++++
3   1 file changed, 8 insertions(+)
```

If there were to be conflicting changes, we'd have to resolve them, just like we did in the previous chapter. And, as we committed things of our own locally, a merge commit has been created. By merging remote/main into main, we won't lose anything we've committed to our local branches. It just updates what we *don't* have, or have, but was changed.

Though, keep in mind that you have to commit your local changes to the local branch, before merging it with the copy of the remote branch.

Now that we're on the same page, we can push our changes back to the remote repository:

```
1  $ git push
```

Now, this was fairly straightforward. Commit a change, fetch the newest data from the remote branch, merge the new state with your own local state, and then push back. However, this is a process that takes multiple commands to finish. In reality, if you're working on a project with multiple people, you'll most likely have new things in the remote repository *constantly*, that you don't have locally.

This means that you'd have to go through this entire process every time someone else made a push - which is tedious and simply annoying.

The pull Command

Git, however, thought about us lazy developers who'd rather avoid this process altogether. It provides us with the pull command. This command fetches the commits to sync up our local branch. Then, it updates the current branch with the commits by performing a merge (by default). Essentially, it automatically does exactly what we did previously manually.

Let's assume our new colleague is a quick one, and pushed yet another update - they added a divide() method to the Calculator.java file.

Now, if we want to sync our local branch with them, we just have got to run the command:

```
1  $ git pull origin main
```

There we go - it fetched the data, synchronized the origin/main branch, and finally merged it into our main branch:

```
1   remote: Enumerating objects: 5, done.
2   remote: Counting objects: 100% (5/5), done.
3   remote: Compressing objects: 100% (1/1), done.
4   remote: Total 3 (delta 2), reused 3 (delta 2), pack\
5   -reused 0
6   Unpacking objects: 100% (3/3), 337 bytes | 337.00 K\
7   iB/s, done.
8   From github.com:dupirefr/calculator
9    * branch            main        -> FETCH_HEAD
10      05a63d1..2afda03  main        -> origin/main
11  Updating 05a63d1..2afda03
12  Fast-forward
13   Calculator.java | 8 ++++++++
14   1 file changed, 8 insertions(+)
```

As we've set up the upstream branch of our local main branch to be the main branch of the remote repository, then a simple git pull would've given us the same result.

Also, the default performed operation is a merge, but we can tell Git to perform a rebase instead by using git pull --rebase. This is a one-shot though, the next pull call without that option will use the merge operation.

If we want the default operation to be a rebase, we've got to tell Git to do so, by altering the local config file:

```
1   $ git config pull.rebase true
```

After that, all pull operations on that repository will perform rebase instead of merge.

Pushing, Fetching and Pulling All Branches

So far, we've been pulling only one specific branch we'd like to sync up with, as well as pushing singular branches to their remote counterparts.

If you're working with a large number of branches, this can also be inconvenient, as you'll have to run the git push and git pull/git fetch commands multiple times.

This can also be automated, and streamlined, using the -all flag, for either of these commands. In all cases, the -all flag simply marks all branches. So if you want to push all the branches to remote, or if you want to pull all branches from remote, you'd do something along the lines of:

```
1  # Pull all branches from origin/remote repository t\
2  o local
3  $ git pull -all origin
4  # Push all local branches to origin/remote reposito\
5  ry
6  $ git push -all origin
```

It's worth noting that you can also use:

```
1  $ git fetch -all origin
```

Though, fetch has its shortcomings because you still have to manually do things. If it was tedious to do things manually for *one* branch, it'll be tedious for multiple branches. It doesn't automatically update local branches (just the remote/origin copies) and it doesn't create new local branches.

This will have to be done manually if you opt to use git fetch, unlike git push which does all of this automatically.

7. Branching Models - Strategies

Now that we know how to deal with remote repositories, it's time we discuss how real collaboration takes place on a software development project that uses Git as its VCS.

In this chapter, we're going to explore a few strategies, called *branching models*, to manage such a project. In the end, we should be able to tell the main benefits and downsides of each model. Also, we should be able to tell if one of those strategies matches the needs of a project we're working on or not.

What's a Branching Model?

For starters, let's define what a *branching model* is, also known as a *branching strategy* or *workflow*.

> A branching model is a series of rules one must follow when working on a software development project to ensure easier collaboration.

In much the same way social etiquette is used to enforce certain behavioral rules, teams all around the world find the best way they can define their workflows to fit their project and team structure. It's called a branching model because it often involves using branches in a certain way, following certain conventions and rules.

Using a branching model is not at all mandatory, but it can facilitate working in parallel on a project, and integrating each other's developed features.

Some models are generally well-known and commonly employed. Some are a lot more niche. Some are variations of more or well-known models. Let's go through some well-known models that you might encounter when working as a collaborator on a project.

Trunk-Based

The first model we're going to talk is the *trunk-based* branching model. This is a simple one. The trunk-based model consists in each contributor committing on the main (or master) branch, often called *the trunk* in other VCSs. Of course, everyone does that on their own copy of the repository. Then, they push their changes to a centralized remote shared by all the contributors.

Branches are allowed. Though, generally, they tend to be short-lived branches[21], maybe up to a few hours, after which it's all brought back to the trunk.

The following picture represents commits on a trunk-based managed repository:

---

[21]https://cloud.google.com/solutions/devops/devops-tech-trunk-based-development

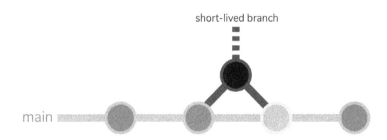

The main advantage of this model is its simplicity. Nobody needs a deep understanding of Git branching and merging/rebasing mechanisms, nor do there have to be sophisticated norms and conventions in regards to making, deleting or maintaining them. Everybody can focus on their work and pile it on the main branch.

Of course, there are disadvantages. The first one is the difficulty to review the code of a given feature. As we're committing on the `main` branch, our code directly melts with other collaborators' code and isolating our own features is more difficult. Even if we work on a short-lived branch, the idea is to merge on the `main` branch before pushing. Thus, if we want our work reviewed by a peer, we must *physically* show it to them.

Also, even though we do officially have a log of all the changes, who made them and when, it's just too cluttered to make much sense. Some of the best advantages of using a distributed VCS completely fade when using this approach.

So, that doesn't work well for remote or distributed teams *at all*.

Note: Code review is the practice of submitting the code we produced to the scrutiny of one or more other developers. They then comment the code to suggest improvements and fixes. Two pairs of eyes are better than one. This leads to software of better quality, ensuring the respect of good programming and software design practices, as well as keeping other team members up to date with the contents of the codebase.

Another disadvantage is the difficulty to deliver features which requires multiple days or weeks to be developed. We can't possibly push unfinished work as it could be picked up for a release. To remedy that, we've got two solutions.

The first one is to push only when we're done. We don't want to do that. Not only can we have a hard disk crash or something of the kind, and lose our work, but also, companies generally set up automated builds and tests to trigger on commits pushed to the remote repository. By working locally, we're missing those which often contain valuable feedback.

So, the second option is to rely on feature toggles[22]. Those are pieces of code that condition our feature's execution (generally being determined by the use of a properties file or a database table). That way, we can push our partially implemented features knowing that they will be disabled in the production environment.

And we can tweak our automated tool chain to build and test the code with and without our features.

With all of the downsides listed, you might ask yourself why someone would employ this model. Just for the sake of simplicity? To *avoid learning about branching*?

No. Trunk-based development found its use in teams that are concerned with *Continuous Integration* and *Continuous Delivery* (CI/CD). On each commit made to the main branch,

---

[22]https://martinfowler.com/articles/feature-toggles.html

a number of automated tests run to make sure that everything still works - not only your commit.

CI/CD wouldn't be able to work at all without a model at least similar to this.

If it works, great! Go on with your day and continue working. If it doesn't work, fix it. To make sure that people don't realize that their code is erroneous *after* they've pushed it, various systems like gated checkins are used to test the code before being pushed.

Then, you can fix things up on your local machine, and push the commit once it's ready.

Feature Branching

The next model is feature branching[23]. Concretely, doing feature branching means creating a branch for each feature developed in an application. Unlike the branches we can create in a trunk-based model, those can, and more than probably will, have a longer life. Once a feature is finished, its branch can be merged back into the main branch, bringing the functionality to it.

The following figure illustrates how a Git repository would look like using feature branching:

---

[23]https://www.atlassian.com/git/tutorials/comparing-workflows/feature-branch-workflow

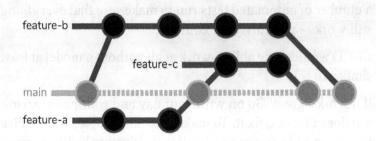

There are a few advantages in choosing this model.

First, we ensure that the main branch contains only finished features, and, most of the time, a releasable version of the code.

Then, we can push those branches to a remote repository. This offers multiple benefits. For starters, we now have the possibility to back up our code somewhere. This means our machine is not the only one to have our version of the code. But also, our code is shared with our collaborators without compromising the main branch, and that leverages its share of advantages too.

Concretely, it means different collaborators can work together on the same feature as they have an easy way to share their work with others.

Nothing's getting merged into main unless it's all stable. This means that merges to main aren't very frequent and each iteration is usually relatively significant.

Also, it makes the code review of a feature much easier. As all the commits dedicated to a feature are on a separate branch, it's pretty easy to get a comparison with the main branch (or any other branch for that matter). Pull requests are making reviewing those changes even easier, but that's a topic for the next section/model!

Of course, there are downsides too. To begin with, setting up an automated tool chain for feature branch can be costly. It multiplies the hardware you need to execute that tool chain. Also, the main branch, is not entirely safe as it contains multiple different features that have been tested separately, but not altogether due to the difficulty of pulling that off. This requires extra effort to test before going to production, and isn't addressed by the model directly. We'll see how the Git Flow strategy takes care of that.

Finally, it's easy to forget updating our feature branches with the main branch, and thus testing our feature based on an outdated codebase.

Moreover, the more behind the main branch we get, the more difficult it can be to merge back. As a lot of files get modified on both sides, more conflicts can occur. And the changes concerned by those conflicts can be old if the branch is a very long-running one, meaning people might not know why the changes were made anymore. This makes conflict resolution much harder.

GitHub Flow

Now, an improvement of the feature branch model is the GitHub Flow[24]. It works exactly like the feature branching model, but *requires* a pull request to be created before merging to the main branch.

A *pull request* is a mechanism offered by GitHub and other Git hosting providers. The purpose is to create a dedicated space for the review of the code of a branch compared to the main

---

[24]https://docs.github.com/en/free-pro-team@latest/github/collaborating-with-issues-and-pull-requests/github-flow

branch. These spaces generally offer a view of the different commits pushed on the branch, plus an overview of all the changes compared to the branch we want to merge to. Finally, a comment system is made available so that collaborators can write notes directly attached to the lines of code.

When the review is finished, the collaborators can directly approve the pull request and the branch is then merged, either manually or by the Git server itself.

To ensure the use of pull requests, the main branch can be locked for push on the server side, preventing anyone to directly push to it.

Compared to feature branching, the big advantage of this model is the ability to comment directly on the code changes. Distributed teams can highly benefit from this asynchronous style of communication. And having the possibility to see a comment right next to the change it concerns avoids wasting time to search the code.

Another feature that often comes with Git servers is the possibility to fork a repository. *Forking* is creating another *remote copy* of a *remote repository*, so we're directly working with *our own remote repository*. When we're finished, we can create pull requests between our remote repository and the original one.

This is common for open-source projects, where people create their own *versions* of a project. For example, comma.ai's[25] open source project, called Openpilot[26] has 4.6k forks as of writing this book. Some of these overhaul many of the features in the Openpilot software, while some of the forks

---

[25]https://comma.ai/
[26]https://github.com/commaai/openpilot

introduce a single changed line, such as, customizing a message that pops up on the UI.

Some of these forks are meant to be *replacements* or *flavors* of the project, which users can use to upload to the comma.ai hardware, replacing the default/official software on it. Some forks are meant to be *improvements* to the official repository, when a third-party collaborator notices something amiss.

The drawbacks of this strategy are pretty much the same as for the feature branching. Although, there is one more - the pull request requirement can be a bit heavy sometimes. Having to review each tiny update, even the shortest one, can be tedious. This is especially true if the `main` branch is locked, therefore preventing the developers to work around the model for such cases.

Git Flow

Finally, let's talk about GitFlow[27]. This is a tough one, because it aims at dealing with a lot of problems encountered on a software development project.

Let's start at the beginning. This model relies on the fact that the `main` branch always represents the latest releasable version. It contains only finished features, that have been tested together, and fixes for bugs that would've been found in production.

Next to that branch is another one, the `develop` branch. This one contains the same code as the `main` branch, plus new features that still haven't made it to `main`. Depending on the

---

[27]https://nvie.com/posts/a-successful-git-branching-model/

team, the develop branch might actually serve as the main branch, while main is reserved for releasable code.

Those features are finished, but not released yet, and have not been entirely tested together. Unfinished features, that are still under development, are implemented on *feature branches*. They are merged back into develop when terminated. To do that, the usage of pull requests is not mandatory, but not forbidden either.

When a set of finished features is ready to be released, a *release* branch is created, generally following the name convention release/x.y.z, where x.y.z is the release version, such as 1.1.2 for example. Often, further tests are conducted on this branch, and some fixes may be needed. They are directly committed on that very branch, and merged back onto develop as needed.

Once a release is ready, its branch is merged into the main branch, but also into develop (to get back the last fixes from the release branch).

At this point, develop and main are in the same state, and the work on the next release can start.

Finally, some bugs may be detected in production, thus on the main branch code. For those bugs, *hotfix* branches are created, generally using the name convention hotfix/x.y.z. They are created from the main branch, and once the fixes look good, they are merged back to the main branch, but also the develop branch, which also needs those fixes.

As an image is worth a thousand words, here is a schema that represents the implementation of the Git Flow model:

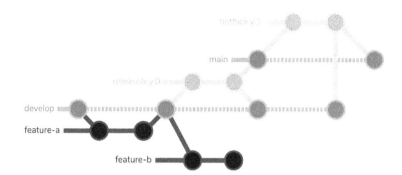

We can see that this model covers a great deal of the aspects of a software development project. This doesn't mean it's the panacea, as stated by the author himself[28]. But, we can say that the model tries to adress most of the problems an organization can encounter developing a project.

And, that's its strength - it addresses a lot of the issues. It offers a main branch that is sacred in the sense that nobody's ever committing directly on it and it always represents the code actually in production. Also, by following the model, we ensure that every fix ever committed is present in the develop branch, which is used by all the collaborators. Finally, all the concerns are well separated, which makes things clear about what is what. A fix of a production problem should be found on a hotfix branch. A fix for a new release should be found on that release branch. Features have their own branches as well.

It also allows setting up automated builds on the develop branch and occasionally on release and hotfix branches, but not for every feature branch.

Of course, its completeness is its own enemy. This flow can be daunting and difficult to master. There are a lot of branches,

---

[28]https://nvie.com/posts/a-successful-git-branching-model/

and developers using such a model should know well how branching works in Git. This model is one of the most popular ones, since it addresses most of the problems seen with other models, but it's also a bit overwhelming for newcomers.

It's nothing too difficult to master, of course, but it still takes some practice and exposure to the environment.

Which One to Choose?

That's an interesting question. And one we won't give an absolute answer here. The fact is - *no model is better than the others*. Each one of them offers advantages and disadvantages. Also, none might suit our particular needs, and each can be improved to better match our specific context.

Trunk-based development is really handy for CI/CD workflows, where changes are constantly being made and pushed. Git Flow is useful for distributed remote teams that deal with slow, substantial updates.

Apart from the Git Flow model, none is offering a way to deal with releases. That doesn't mean that we need to use Git Flow, we can just start from a model and decide how releases will be handled in our specific case. A lot of these conventions are soft - you discuss the requirements with your team, figure out a way that works for everyone, and settle for that.

Additionally, there's no need to stick to just one model throughout the entire life of the project. You can start out with a trunk-based model, making quick progress towards a state that you can demonstrate to others. And then, once you get to a certain point and start getting more people onboard, switch to something more akin to the Git Flow model.

Here are a few questions that can help us in determining the best strategy[29] (or the one that addresses the most our needs before being tweaked according to your desires):

- Do we need to deliver features very quickly? Then the simplest model, with the least branches possible, would probably meet our needs.
- Do we need to enforce code reviews? Then a model with pull requests might suit us more.
- Is our team skilled with using Git? Then we can consider more complex models. Otherwise, the trunk-based model might be better for us.
- Generally, are we developing features in hours or in days or weeks? Longer features might require their own branches, thus taking the trunk-based model out of the equation.
- Are we working with senior or junior developers? More senior developers might require less structure than juniors.

This is not an exhaustive list of questions, more can certainly be asked to choose a model. It gives us somewhere to start.

The goal here is to find the model that will match our expectations the best. And that may require a few changes to the existing models, let's not forget that.

---

[29]https://www.toptal.com/software/trunk-based-development-git-flow

8. Advanced Operations

We're starting to have a really good grasp of how to use Git properly. We know the commands used to work with the local repository and branches therein, how to interact with remote repositories and branches, and how to collaborate effectively with other people through the use of branching models.

So, now, we'll talk about a few Git operations we didn't mention before. Those are more advanced, less commonly used operations, compared to the basic add, commit, pull and push operations.

Although they're not as commonly used as the first category, they're nonetheless important and very useful when it comes to working with Git.

We'll cover a few new operations in this chapter:

- The stash operation that allows us to save uncommitted changes, for later reuse, in a dedicated space of the repository.

- The tag operation which allows us to label a commit to retrieve it easier, instead of using commit hashes.

- The reset and revert operations, for when we're not happy with the work we've currently achieved and want to rollback some modifications.

- The `cherry-pick` operation, which allows us to copy the content of a single cherry-picked commit of another branch. A practical, but risky way of selectively picking and applying changes from another branch.
- The `git diff` operation, which allows us to take a look and compare differences between files.
- The `commit --amend` operation, which allows us to modify the latest commit.
- We'll see how to perform an *interactive rebase*, which is a fine-grained version of the rebase we already know.
- Finally, we'll take a look at how to perform *interactive staging*, which is also a fine-grained version of staging files like we usually do.

Along the way, we'll get bits and pieces about other useful Git commands like `show` or `diff`, but also *Git references*.

Stash

Let's start with stashing! Stashing changes means we put them aside for potential later reuse. Let's imagine the following scenario: we're working on a new feature for our Calculator, but as it's a quick one, we're working directly on the `main` branch. Making a new feature branch for it would be an overkill.

Then, our manager comes to see us because there is an *urgent* bug to fix in production.

What do we do then? We already have a few changes with the new feature that are not ready to go into production, and we have to *quickly* tackle that bug. We *stash* the changes made so far, fix the bug, and then go back to the feature once it's done.

The git stash command takes all the tracked changes and put them in a dedicated area - .git/refs/stash. Once the working directory and index are stashed away, the project reverts to the latest HEAD commit, before we made the changes with the new feature. Each stash is piled up on a stack, but only the latest one is stored in this stash file and it resides until we explicitly clear it.

Once a new stash replaces the old one, the previous stash is added to the reflog file of that ref. We'll talk about references and reference logs a bit later in this chapter. For now - the latest stash is stored in the stash file, while the older stashes are stored in the log/stack.

Let's see concretely how the stash operation works, by first taking a look at the current state of our repository:

```
1  $ git status
2  On branch main
3  Your branch and 'origin/main' have diverged,
4  and have 2 and 1 different commits each, respective\
5  ly.
6    (use "git pull" to merge the remote branch into y\
7  ours)
8
9  Changes not staged for commit:
10   (use "git add <file>..." to update what will be c\
11 ommitted)
12   (use "git restore <file>..." to discard changes i\
13 n working directory)
14        modified:   Calculator.java
15
16 no changes added to commit (use "git add" and/or "g\
17 it commit -a")
```

We've modified our `Calculator.java` file, and it's not yet staged for commit. Let's put aside those changes using `git stash`:

```
1   $ git stash
```

This results in:

```
1   Saved working directory and index state WIP on main\
2   : 537e61d Added information about the project colla\
3   borators
```

You can also see our latest commit there. The HEAD is set back to the latest commit we've made, which was the one where we added information about project collaborators.

The `git stash` command itself is a shortcut for the regular syntax - `git stash push`. If we use the full syntax, we can also give a name to our stash, by providing an `-m` flag:

```
1   $ git stash push -m "subtraction_for_doubles"
```

All of our stashes are saved, until cleared. The latest one is in the stash file for the convenience of retrieval, though, we can easily access all of them via the `git stash list` command:

```
1   stash@{0}: On main: subtraction_for_doubles
```

We can see that stashes are numbered. As the stash area is a stack, each new stash is attributed with the index of 0, while the others being shifted. If we add another stash, the `subtraction_for_doubles` stash would be indexed with 1.

Once we've fixed the urgent bug and pushed the change to main, we can go back to our work on the feature. To do that, we'll retrieve it from the stash via the git stash pop command.

This reinstates the last stashed changes, reintroducing our changes we stashed before, and removes it from the stack:

```
On branch main
Your branch and 'origin/main' have diverged,
and have 2 and 1 different commits each, respective\
ly.
  (use "git pull" to merge the remote branch into y\
ours)

Changes not staged for commit:
  (use "git add <file>..." to update what will be c\
ommitted)
  (use "git restore <file>..." to discard changes i\
n working directory)
        modified:   Calculator.java

no changes added to commit (use "git add" and/or "g\
it commit -a")
Dropped refs/stash@{0} (8d6f8c9ae385802613f4a4ed950\
b6d5047e39bb3)
```

Now, if we run:

```
$ git stash list
```

We're greeted with an empty list:

Alternatively, you can use `git stash apply` to unstash the change, and still keep it in the list.

Now, let's go back and see what was going on under the hood back here when we added and removed the stashes.

Since we're on a clean slate again, let's add a file, just to play around with the `stash` command:

```
$ touch stashfile.txt
$ git add stashfile.txt
```

The status is:

```
On branch main
Changes to be committed:
  (use "git reset HEAD <file>..." to unstage)

        new file:   stashfile.txt
```

Now, let's stash this file away:

```
$ git stash push -m "Adding stashfile.txt to the st\
ash"
Saved working directory and index state On master: \
Adding stashfile.txt to the stash
```

Now, let's create another file and stash it away too:

```
1  $ touch secondstashfile.txt
2  $ git add secondstashfile.txt
3  $ git stash push -m "Adding secondstashfile.txt to \
4  the stash"
```

This also results in:

```
1  Saved working directory and index state On master: \
2  Adding secondstashfile.txt to the stash
```

Now, if we run git stash list:

```
1  $ git stash list
2  stash@{0}: On master: Adding secondstashfile.txt to\
3   the stash
4  stash@{1}: On master: Adding stashfile.txt to the s\
5  tash
```

The stash on the 0th index is located in the .git/refs/stash file.
The stash on the 1st index is located under .git/logs/refs/stash.

Let's take a look at those files now:

```
1  $ cd .git/refs
2  $ ls -a
3  ./  ../  heads/  stash  tags/
```

There it is! Let's open it in a text editor:

```
1  $ nano stash
```

It contains:

```
1  4e6ecd4ac146e29be1c8f1a5c1dd094baee65e14
```

So, the entire `stash` file is just used to save the hash for the latest stash. Let's navigate to the other folder and take a look at the other stash we've saved:

```
1  $ cd ..
2  $ cd logs/refs
3  $ ls -a
4  ./  ../  heads/  stash
```

Now, this is where our reference logs are stored. And specifically, the stashes older than the latest one are stored in *this* stash file:

```
1  $ nano stash
2
3  0000000000000000000000000000000000000000 77a327e29c\
4  46df8b1c9cde9208ef681eaebc52>
5  77a327e29c46df8b1c9cde9208ef681eaebc52ab 4e6ecd4ac1\
6  46e29be1c8f1a5c1dd094baee65e>
```

Originally, no stash hash was present, which was followed with the `77a327` hash. Then, that hash was followed by the newest `4e6ecd` hash.

This isn't of too much use to us, as it's what Git keeps track of under the hood for a reason. You aren't really required or supposed to dabble with these files - though, it does help visualize what's going on.

Once we're ready to unstash some older stashes, we can do so with `git stash apply` or `git stash pop`:

```
1   $ git stash list
2   stash@{0}: On master: Adding secondstashfile.txt to\
3    the stash
4   stash@{1}: On master: Adding stashfile.txt to the s\
5   tash
6
7   $ git stash pop
8   On branch master
9   Changes to be committed:
10    (use "git restore --staged <file>..." to unstage)
11          new file:   secondstashfile.txt
12
13  Dropped refs/stash@{0} (4e6ecd4ac146e29be1c8f1a5c1d\
14  d094baee65e14)
15
16  $ git stash apply
17  On branch master
18  Changes to be committed:
19    (use "git restore --staged <file>..." to unstage)
20          new file:   secondstashfile.txt
21          new file:   stashfile.txt
```

Tag

Let's move on to an easy one - *tagging*.

Creating Tags and Tagging Commits

Tagging is the operation of assigning a label to a commit, making it easier to find in the whole repository history. Generally, the commits that are tagged have a special meaning.

For example, it's a relatively common practice to tag commits from which releases are made.

You can tag each and every commit, though, that might very well be overkill. Generally, you can use tagging to *highlight* certain commits over other ones. To tag a commit, you simply run the git tag command, followed by the tag name. The tag name cannot use double quotation marks, but can use single quotation marks:

```
1  $ git tag finished-division-feature
2  $ git tag 'ready for release 0.1.0'
```

We can put multiple tags on a commit. For example, we've added these two tags to our latest commit. Now if we check the latest commit with git log -1:

```
1  commit 2afda03076d9a02fc864cf074773a0845bbed07e (HE\
2  AD -> main, tag: ready for release 0.1.0, tag: fini\
3  shed-division-feature, origin/main)
4  Author: collaborator <francois.dupire@nerthusconsul\
5  ting.be>
6  Date:   Sun Dec 13 21:07:42 2020 +0100
7
8      Added a division feature as well
```

We can see two tags readily available after the branch name. Your terminal will likely color-highlight these tags differently so that they're very easily noticeable.

Since we can add more tags by using the command again - we must use different names each time. Each tag must be unique in the repository. Finally, we can delete a tag by using the -d option of the command:

```
1  $ git tag -d finished-division-feature
2  Deleted tag 'finished-division-featuret' (was 537e6\
3  1d)
4
5  $ git tag -d 'ready for release 0.1.0'
6  Deleted tag 'finished-division-featuret' (was 2gfd5\
7  2h)
```

Now, there is one more thing to know about tags. The ones we created so far are merely labels, as you might expect them to be. Although, it's possible to create a tag that's a totally separate Git object, like commits are. Those are called *annotated tags*, and we must associate a message to them as we do with commits.

To create one, we must use the -a option, as well as -m for the message:

```
1  $ git tag -a release/0.1.0 -m "Calculator Beta"
```

In addition to having a message, this tag also has an author and a timestamp. We can confirm that using a new Git command, git show release/0.1.0:

```
1  tag release/0.1.0
2  Tagger: francois <francois.dupire@nerthusconsulting\
3  .be>
4  Date:   Sun Dec 13 21:30:43 2020 +0100
5
6  Calculator Beta
7
8  commit 2afda03076d9a02fc864cf074773a0845bbed07e (HE\
9  AD -> main, tag: release/0.1.0, origin/main)
```

```
10  Author: collaborator <francois.dupire@nerthusconsul\
11  ting.be>
12  Date:    Sun Dec 13 21:07:42 2020 +0100
13
14      Added a division feature as well
15
16  diff --git a/Calculator.java b/Calculator.java
17  index 843b685..1af39e2 100644
18  --- a/Calculator.java
19  +++ b/Calculator.java
20  @@ -14,4 +14,12 @@ public class Calculator {
21      public double mutiply(double a, double b) {
22        return a * b;
23      }
24  +
25  +   public int divide(int a, int b) {
26  +     return a / b;
27  +   }
28  +
29  +   public double divide(double a, double b) {
30  +     return a / b;
31  +   }
32    }
```

We can see that the command outputs a lot of information. First, it prints out the data of the tag (name, author, timestamp and message). After that, we've got information about the associated commit, including a git diff for that commit. This could've been printed using git diff HEAD^, though, we'll talk about this a bit later in this chapter.

Listing out tags is as easy as using the git tag command:

```
1  $ git tag
2  release/0.1.0
```

The tags are sorted alphabetically, and you can open each one if you'd like as shown in the previous paragraphs.

Now, we've been tagging the *latest* commit only. What happens if we forget to tag something? You can tag *any* commit by providing a shortened hash for it. Let's check our log and pick out another commit that might be worth tagging retroactively:

```
1  $ git log
2
3  ...
4  commit d6753cb4d15ed30815b480fbf1c5c8abc6a63ca1 (HE\
5  AD -> main)
6  Author: francois <francois.dupire@nerthusconsulting\
7  .be>
8  Date:    Sat Jan 2 22:58:19 2021 +0100
9
10     Initial commit
```

This is the first commit we've made in the book. Let's use that:

```
1  $ git tag -a release/0.0.0 d6753cb -m "Release 0.0.\
2  0"
```

And now, let's list them again:

```
1  $ git tag
2  release/0.0.0
3  release/0.1.0
```

Note: Tags aren't pushed to the remote repository by default, alongside their commits. They need to be pushed themselves, manually, totally regardless of the commits themselves. We can do this alongside the commits, or retroactively.

Pushing Tags

Let's go ahead and push our tag to origin:

```
1  $ git push origin release/0.0.0
2  Enumerating objects: 1, done.
3  Counting objects: 100% (1/1), done.
4  Writing objects: 100% (1/1), 174 bytes | 174.00 KiB\
5  /s, done.
6  Total 1 (delta 0), reused 0 (delta 0), pack-reused 0
7  To https://github.com/dupirefr/calculator
8   * [new tag]        release/0.0.0 -> release/0.0.0
```

Now, our remote repository also contains the tag, if we check the initial commit:

Also, we can now navigate to that tag:

Now, we pushed only one tag. If you went back and tagged a bunch of your important commits, you'll want to push them all together, rather than one by one.

This can easily be done via `git push --tags`:

```
1  $ git push --tags
2  Enumerating objects: 1, done.
3  Counting objects: 100% (1/1), done.
4  Writing objects: 100% (1/1), 176 bytes | 176.00 KiB\
5  /s, done.
6  Total 1 (delta 0), reused 0 (delta 0), pack-reused 0
7  To https://github.com/dupirefr/calculator
8   * [new tag]          release/0.1.0 -> release/0.1.0
```

We've also got the `release/0.1.0` tag, which is now pushed to the remote as well.

Checking Out Tags

As with branches and commits, you can also `git checkout` tags to return to that state again:

```
1  $ git checkout release/0.0.0
```

This results in:

```
1  $ git checkout release/0.0.0
2  Note: switching to 'release/0.0.0'.
3
4  You are in 'detached HEAD' state. You can look arou\
5  nd, make experimental
6  changes and commit them, and you can discard any co\
7  mmits you make in this
8  state without impacting any branches by switching b\
9  ack to a branch.
10
11 If you want to create a new branch to retain commit\
12 s you create, you may
13 do so (now or later) by using -c with the switch co\
14 mmand. Example:
15
16   git switch -c <new-branch-name>
17
18 Or undo this operation with:
19
20   git switch -
21
22 Turn off this advice by setting config variable adv\
23 ice.detachedHead to false
24
25 HEAD is now at d6753cb Initial commit
```

Since we can't really change the foundational building blocks
that are far gone behind us, we're in a "detached HEAD"
state. This means that we can work and commit without really

committing. Once we're finished, we can either create a new branch for this to avoid affecting old ones, or we can start off by creating a new branch for these tests.

Let's go back to our current commit and tag:

```
1  $ git checkout release/0.1.0
2  Previous HEAD position was d6753cb Initial commit
3  HEAD is now at 2afda03 adding new file
```

Note: While you're switching around like this, you're still working with a detached head. This won't change until you change it explicitly yourself. Even going back to the latest release won't return the HEAD back.

To delete the changes associated to the detached head, and just go back to main, all you have to do is:

```
1  $ git checkout main
2  Switched to branch 'main'
3  Your branch is up to date with 'origin/main'.
```

And if you want to keep them, you'll have to make a new branch and then you can switch back to main:

```
1  # Creates temporary and saves the changes to it
2  $ git branch temporary
3  $ git checkout main
4  Switched to branch 'main'
5  Your branch is up to date with 'origin/main'.
```

Reset

Now, let's talk about the reset operation. The purpose of this operation is to reset the current branch back to a certain commit.

If we inspect the division feature code, we can see it doesn't manage the zero denominator corner case. That's pretty bad, so we decide to reset the main branch to the commit before that, that is HEAD^.

Here is our current history:

```
 1  git log --oneline
 2  2afda03 (HEAD -> main, tag: release/0.1.0, origin/m\
 3  ain) Added a division feature as well
 4  05a63d1 Merge remote-tracking branch 'origin/main' \
 5  into main
 6  c367c20 Added information about the project collabo\
 7  rators
 8  ba2c556 Added a feature to multiply integer and dec\
 9  imal number
10  3649cab Added explanation about the remote reposito\
11  ry
12  c776831 Added Application to call the Calculator
13  225a7d7 Merge branch 'feature/addition'
14  0e5cddc Implemented decimal addition on a branch
15  e60f380 Merge branch 'feature/addition'
16  d2d817c Added an entry in CHANGELOG about new featu\
17  re
18  080d442 Implemented decimal addition on master
19  e700e3f Implemented integer addition
20  efb51ef Ignored my personal To Do list
```

```
21   33df91c Extra information about the project, a chan\
22   gelog file and our future Calculator class file
23   dd11b5b Added project title to the README
24   d6753cb Initial commit
```

Here, we used another option of the git log command: --oneline. This tells Git to print only the (reduced) hash of the commits as well as the first line of their message. As our history is starting to become big, it's coming in as a handy option.

If we want to get rid of commit 2afda03, and go back to an older one, we'll locate where we want to go to and *reset* to that point.

For example, we can reset to 05a63d1 to practically revert the latest commit:

```
1   $ git reset 05a63d1
```

Git then tells us we've unstaged changes after the operation:

```
1   Unstaged changes after reset:
2   M        Calculator.java
```

Concretely, that means that our changes are not lost, but merely un-committed. We can then decide what to do with them: *discard them, make some changes*, etc.

Discarding Changes

If we want to make sure that those changes are discarded, even before executing the reset operation, we'd use the --hard flag.

Git will discard the changes in addition to resetting the branch to the given commit, when the --hard flag is used.

Here is the result of executing a git reset --hard 05a63d1:

```
1  $ git reset --hard 05a63d1
2  HEAD is now at 05a63d1 Merge remote-tracking branch\
3   'origin/main' into main
```

A git status will confirm us there are no more detected changes, but that it's behind origin/main by 1 commit, since we've removed the latest commit from our local branch:

```
1  $ git status
2  On branch main
3  Your branch is behind 'origin/main' by 1 commit, an\
4  d can be fast-forwarded.
5    (use "git pull" to update your local branch)
6
7  nothing to commit, working tree clean
```

In addition to the --hard option, the reset operation also offers the --soft and --mixed options. The former ensures that the changes will stay in the staging area after the reset, while the latter is the default behavior - thus removing the commits, but keeping the changes unstaged.

Force Pushing

What if we had already pushed some commits to the remote repository? We have, and we're behind the remote repository by this one commit that we've effectively lost by resetting to an earlier one.

Then Git won't let us push as if nothing happened, we'll have to force it to accept our branch as is by using the --force or --force-with-lease options.

Let's try pushing again after we've reset back to a commit before the latest one:

```
$ git push
To https://github.com/dupirefr/calculator
 ! [rejected]        main -> main (non-fast-forward)
error: failed to push some refs to 'https://github.\
com/dupirefr/calculator'
hint: Updates were rejected because the tip of your\
 current branch is behind
hint: its remote counterpart. Integrate the remote \
changes (e.g.
hint: 'git pull ...') before pushing again.
hint: See the 'Note about fast-forwards' in 'git pu\
sh --help' for details.
```

However, if we wanted to force push our current state, and *really* delete the latest commit, we could do so by running the push command with the --force or --force-with-lease flags.

Those options tell Git that our version of the branch must erase the remote one. The second option, though, is safer because it checks that the remote reference is the same as the one in our matching tracking branch:

```
1  $ git push --force-with-lease
2  Total 0 (delta 0), reused 0 (delta 0), pack-reused 0
3  To https://github.com/dupirefr/calculator
4   + 2afda03...05a63d1 main -> main (forced update)
```

This means we only erase changes on the remote branch if nothing more was committed to it since we last pushed.

We should always be careful before forcing our changes onto a remote branch as we might erase somebody else's work, or even our own. In general, forced changes aren't common, and forcing your change can both be seen in a negative light by colleagues, as well as a lack of will to work on your own copy of the project to make sure you conform with everyone else.

Please make sure that you communicate with your team before using a forced push.

Revert

Sometimes, resetting our branch is not an option. If we pushed our commits a long time ago, we can't just reset the branch and discard other, valid commits as well. If we did, we'd be overkilling it for a simple change - why not just make the change in the file and commit it at that point again, instead of rewriting old commits? In these cases, we can use `revert`.

Reverting a commit means creating another commit that contains exactly the *opposite* changes of the original commit. It's a way of discarding changes of a commit without rewriting a branch's history.

Let's say we're not happy that our new collaborator committed work on multiplication without asking us for a code review.

Let's check our history again:

```
1   $ git log --oneline
2   05a63d1 (HEAD -> main) Merge remote-tracking branch\
3    'origin/main' into main
4   c367c20 Added information about the project collabo\
5   rators
6   ba2c556 Added a feature to multiply integer and dec\
7   imal number
8   3649cab Added explanation about the remote reposito\
9   ry
10  c776831 Added Application to call the Calculator
11  225a7d7 Merge branch 'feature/addition'
12  0e5cddc Implemented decimal addition on a branch
13  e60f380 Merge branch 'feature/addition'
14  d2d817c Added an entry in CHANGELOG about new featu\
15  re
16  080d442 Implemented decimal addition on master
17  e700e3f Implemented integer addition
18  efb51ef Ignored my personal To Do list
19  33df91c Extra information about the project, a chan\
20  gelog file and our future Calculator class file
21  dd11b5b Added project title to the README
22  d6753cb Initial commit
```

The commit to revert is the ba2c556. This is where the sneaky colleague pushed without asking for a code review. Now, we can follow our usual convention and just write git revert ba2c556. Though, we could also write:

```
1   $ git revert HEAD^^
```

The usage of HEAD^^ tells Git to select the commit before the commit that's located before HEAD. Since that sentence was a

mouthful - adding ^ to any Git reference can be translated by
"the one before that". So, if we wanted to target the commit
before the current one, we could've used HEAD^. Two commits
down the line would be HEAD^^, three commits down the line
would be HEAD^^^, etc.

This becomes tedious if we want to select a commit further in
history. So, there is another notation that allows us to specify
which commit before HEAD we want: HEAD@{x}. x being the
number of commits to go back in history. Here, it'd have been
HEAD@{2}.

Let's run this command now. Our editor opens with a prede-
fined commit message - Revert "commit message". Once you
save the message, a new commit has been made:

```
1  [main 90ff63e] Revert "Added a feature to multiply \
2  integer and decimal number"
3   1 file changed, 2 deletions(-)
```

Of course, now our changes have been removed from the
working tree, and we haven't affected other pieces of the
codebase.

Revert can be very practical when one of our commits causes
failure on an automated toolchain and we don't have time to
investigate further right away. And it's a rather safe operation
as nothing is lost. The original commit is still in the history,
so we can retrieve the changes if needed.

Now, our log contains this new commit as well:

```
1  $ git log --oneline
2  90ff63e (HEAD -> main) Revert "Added a feature to m\
3  ultiply integer and decimal number"
4  05a63d1 Merge remote-tracking branch 'origin/main' \
5  into main
6  c367c20 Added information about the project collabo\
7  rators
8  ba2c556 Added a feature to multiply integer and dec\
9  imal number
10 3649cab Added explanation about the remote reposito\
11 ry
12 c776831 Added Application to call the Calculator
13 225a7d7 Merge branch 'feature/addition'
14 0e5cddc Implemented decimal addition on a branch
15 e60f380 Merge branch 'feature/addition'
16 d2d817c Added an entry in CHANGELOG about new featu\
17 re
18 080d442 Implemented decimal addition on master
19 e700e3f Implemented integer addition
20 efb51ef Ignored my personal To Do list
21 33df91c Extra information about the project, a chan\
22 gelog file and our future Calculator class file
23 dd11b5b Added project title to the README
24 d6753cb Initial commit
```

Furthermore, we can just revert our revert commit if we want! Let's revert HEAD, since that's the latest commit:

```
1   $ git revert HEAD
2   [main 99e1eeb] Revert "Revert "Added explanation ab\
3   out the remote repository""
4    1 file changed, 2 insertions(+)
5
6   $ git log --oneline
7   99e1eeb (HEAD -> main) Revert "Revert "Added explan\
8   ation about the remote repository""
9   90ff63e Revert "Added explanation about the remote \
10  repository"
11  c367c20 (origin/main, origin/HEAD) Added informatio\
12  n about the project collaborators
13  ...
```

Now, our working directory is in the state before we reverted
it for the first time.

Revert Conflicts

Of course, when you're dabbling with history (albeit, not
directly, we're applying an inverse change in the future, not
rewriting history) like this, you might very well run into a
conflict. For example, we can easily revert the last change to
our Calculator.java file, since nothing was done on it after
that.

However, if we want to revert an older commit on it, after
which, someone else committed changes to this file again,
we're greeted with a familiar message.

Let's run the log again:

```
1  $ git log --oneline
2  # Shortened for brevity
3  ...
4  e700e3f Implemented integer addition
5  efb51ef Ignored my personal To Do list
6  33df91c Extra information about the project, a chan\
7  gelog file and our future Calculator class file
8  dd11b5b Added project title to the README
9  d6753cb Initial commit
```

If we dabble with the e700e3f commit, which introduced integer addition, we'll be making a conflict, since further down the line, we've made further changes to the Calculator.java file.

Let's try reverting to it:

```
1   $ git revert e700e3f
2   Auto-merging Calculator.java
3   CONFLICT (content): Merge conflict in Calculator.ja\
4   va
5   error: could not revert e700e3f... Implemented inte\
6   ger addition
7   hint: after resolving the conflicts, mark the corre\
8   cted paths
9   hint: with 'git add <paths>' or 'git rm <paths>'
10  hint: and commit the result with 'git commit'
```

Now, you'll have to resolve this conflict, --skip the patch or --abort the revert:

```
 1   $ git status
 2   On branch main
 3
 4   You are currently reverting commit e700e3f.
 5     (fix conflicts and run "git revert --continue")
 6     (use "git revert --skip" to skip this patch)
 7     (use "git revert --abort" to cancel the revert op\
 8   eration)
 9
10   Unmerged paths:
11     (use "git restore --staged <file>..." to unstage)
12     (use "git add <file>..." to mark resolution)
13           both modified:    Calculator.java
14
15   no changes added to commit (use "git add" and/or "g\
16   it commit -a")
```

If you have multiple commits to revert, you can --skip this one. Since we're doing only one, --skip and --abort will have the same impact:

```
 1   $ git revert --abort
```

Cherry-pick

The next in line is the *cherry-pick* operation. Let's say we are working on a feature branch, but a part of the code we produced there is needed on the main branch. We can't possibly merge the branch now, it's not production-ready. One part of the work is done and works as expected, but we can't push the rest yet. Then, the solution is to *cherry-pick* the commit of our branch that's ready, and push it to main.

Then, we can continue working on the rest of the features until they're ready and push them at a later date.

But, what's *cherry-picking* a commit? Concretely, it's creating another commit that applies exactly the same changes as the one you picked.

Now, how do we cherry-pick a commit? Let's say we create a feature/subtraction branch and commit two changes: subtraction for integers and for decimal numbers.

Then we're told that subtraction for integers is urgently needed in production. Thus, we get the hash of the first commit and get back on the main branch to perform the cherry-pick:

```
$ git cherry-pick 98ec667
```

Git thus creates another commit with the integer subtraction, under a new hash, for main:

```
[main 22fdfc7] Implemented subtraction for integers
 Date: Sun Dec 13 21:53:16 2020 +0100
 1 file changed, 4 insertions(+)
```

The drawback of this technique is that it creates an entirely different commit, with another hash, making it impossible for Git to know that those commits are related. Let's say we want to see what are the commits on feature/subtraction that are not on main:

```
git log --oneline feature/subtraction ^main
```

This time we passed some arguments to the git log command. Those are branches, but any Git reference will do.

By passing a reference to that command, we want to see the history of that particular branch. Here, we are passing two branches, but used the ^ character in front of one, meaning we want the commit history of the first branch, but only those that are not in the second.

As a matter of fact, the command takes a revision range. The documentation provides a great short guide to specifying ranges[30].

This will outputs the following:

```
1   7c51980 (feature/subtraction) Implemented subtracti\
2   on for doubles
3   98ec667 Implemented subtraction for integers
```

So, here is the commit with the decimal subtraction feature, but also the one we cherry-picked.

Furthermore, if we try to merge the feature/subtraction branch into main Git will tell us there is a conflict in the Calculator.java file. Effectively, it's as if two developers committed work on that file (even though it's not the case).

Since it's essentially the same change, you can either keep the one from main or override it with your own. Assuming that someone could've changed that file again after you've cherry-picked it, you might want to keep the main version.

This is one of the disadvantages of using cherry-pick. And it's not too hard to imagine other issues that could arise

---

[30]https://git-scm.com/docs/gitrevisions#_specifying_ranges

from cherry-picking one commit, from a list of commits and pushing it to another branch.

Many find cherry-picking to be bad practice in general, and many find it useful. In fact, Raymond Chen wrote an entire *series of articles*[31] on why you *shouldn't cherry-pick* and why you should merge instead.

Git Diffs

The `git diff` command is a really useful command that lets us preview changes (or differences) between references - such as commits and branches, as well as files

Git Diff on Files

For example, let's add a new line to our `CHANGELOG.md` file, and call `git diff` on it, before we add that change to our staging area:

```
1  $ echo "Another change" >> CHANGELOG.md
2
3  $ git diff CHANGELOG.md
4  diff --git a/CHANGELOG.md b/CHANGELOG.md
5  index 4fdcb53..252c307 100644
6  --- a/CHANGELOG.md
7  +++ b/CHANGELOG.md
8  @@ -1,3 +1,4 @@
9   # 2020-12-11
10   * Added a decimal addition feature
11   * Added an integer addition feature
12  +Another change
```

---

[31]https://devblogs.microsoft.com/oldnewthing/20180323-01/?p=98325

As you can see, we've got a/CHANGELOG.md and b/CHANGELOG.md, which represent our file in the previously recorded and current state. If we add the file to the index, that state will be the latest recorded state and git diff wouldn't print anything.

Additionally, between the @@ symbols, we can see that the original file had 3 lines, whereas the new file has 4 lines. Compared to each other, the former version has -1 lines, and the new version has +1 line.

The little + before Another change is the line that we added. Other lines, are left as they were, without any prefixes.

Once we add this file though, we can't see these changes using git diff anymore:

```
1  $ git add CHANGELOG.md
2  $ git diff CHANGELOG.md
3  # Empty...
```

However, we can still access this diff by using the --cached flag, so we compare the index with the local repository, instead of the HEAD:

```
1   $ git diff --cached CHANGELOG.md
2   diff --git a/CHANGELOG.md b/CHANGELOG.md
3   index 4fdcb53..252c307 100644
4   --- a/CHANGELOG.md
5   +++ b/CHANGELOG.md
6   @@ -1,3 +1,4 @@
7   # 2020-12-11
8    * Added a decimal addition feature
9    * Added an integer addition feature
10  +Another change
```

Additionally, you can check the entire index or HEAD by providing the adequate references to `git diff`. Let's add another file again, add it to the index and run the commands again:

```
1   $ touch newfile
2   $ git add newfile
3   $ git diff HEAD
4   diff --git a/CHANGELOG.md b/CHANGELOG.md
5   index 4fdcb53..252c307 100644
6   --- a/CHANGELOG.md
7   +++ b/CHANGELOG.md
8   @@ -1,3 +1,4 @@
9    # 2020-12-11
10    * Added a decimal addition feature
11    * Added an integer addition feature
12   +Another change
13   diff --git a/newfile b/newfile
14   new file mode 100644
15   index 0000000..e69de29
16
17   $ git diff --cached
18   diff --git a/CHANGELOG.md b/CHANGELOG.md
19   index 4fdcb53..252c307 100644
20   --- a/CHANGELOG.md
21   +++ b/CHANGELOG.md
22   @@ -1,3 +1,4 @@
23    # 2020-12-11
24    * Added a decimal addition feature
25    * Added an integer addition feature
26   +Another change
27   diff --git a/newfile b/newfile
28   new file mode 100644
```

```
29    index 0000000..e69de29
```

Git Diff on Commits

So far, we've been comparing the differences between two states of a file before and after it's been added to the index. Now, let's compare the difference between two commits of a same file. For example, let's compare the difference between the commit that added the decimal addition feature, and the commit that added the integer addition feature.

First, we'll locate them:

```
1    $ git log --oneline
2    ...
```

Then, we'll use `git diff` on their shortened hashes:

```
1    $ git diff e700e3f 080d442
2    diff --git a/Calculator.java b/Calculator.java
3    index 32e8410..c01b9c0 100644
4    --- a/Calculator.java
5    +++ b/Calculator.java
6    @@ -2,4 +2,8 @@ public class Calculator {
7        public int addition(int a, int b) {
8          return a + b;
9        }
10   +
11   +   public double addition(double a, double b) {
12   +     return a + b;
13   +   }
14     }
```

Git Diff on Branches

We can also check diffs between branches this way. Let's make a new branch from the main branch, and make some changes there. Then, we'll run git diff to take a look at these changes:

```
1  $ git checkout main
2  $ git branch new-branch
3  $ git checkout new-branch
4  $ touch new-branch-file.txt
5  $ echo "A new line in a new file" >> new-branch-fil\
6  e.txt
7  $ git add new-branch-file.txt
8  $ git commit -m "Added new file"
9  $ git diff main new-branch
10 diff --git a/new-branch-file.txt b/new-branch-file.\
11 txt
12 new file mode 100644
13 index 0000000..a4fd187
14 --- /dev/null
15 +++ b/new-branch-file.txt
16 @@ -0,0 +1 @@
17 +A new line in a new file
```

If we switch the branches around, the diff will essentially be the opposite. From the context of main, this was an added file. If we compared git diff new-branch main, Git would tell us that we've *removed* the new-branch-file and its contents, since it's present in the new-branch, but not in main.

Amending Commits

A great and neat little trick to changing previous commits is amending. Made a typo in the last message? Forgot to note something you did?

Using git commit --amend, you can edit the last commit:

```
1   $ git commit --amend -m "Fixed bug, but also change\
2   d line..."
```

By amending a commit with the -m flag, we update its message, but the hash stays the same.

Now, you might also forget to add some change as well. Instead of making a new commit, you can also edit the previous one to include new files or changes as well:

```
1   $ touch newfile
2   $ git add newfile
3   $ git commit --amend -m "Fixed bug, changed line...\
4    and also added a new file!"
```

This will overwrite your old commit with a new one, with a new hash, of course, and replace the old one:

```
1   [main be07888] Fixed bug, changed line... and also \
2   added a new file!
3    Date: Sun Jan 10 21:46:09 2021 +0100
4    2 files changed, 0 insertions(+), 0 deletions(-)
5    create mode 100644 newfile
```

Now, you can only ever `--amend` the latest commit. You can't go before that using this command. However, you can rewrite older history and pick certain commits to change using *interactive rebasing*.

Interactive Rebase

We've already covered what a rebase is in *"Chapter 5 - Branches"* : it's reapplying commits of a branch on top of another branch or Git reference. Typically, all the commits that are on the current branch and not in the history of the other references are reapplied.

In an interactive rebase, we can decide to perform dedicated actions for each commit. We'll cover a few commonly used ones here.

First, let's see how to start an interactive rebase. Imagine we've added a third commit on our `feature/subtraction` branch that refactored both implementations a bit. Now, say we want to start an interactive rebase for all the commits of that branch.

Then, we've got to rebase on the commit before the first new one. This time around, we'll also use a `-i` flag, to start the *interactive* mode:

```
$ git rebase -i b4bdab6
```

Our editor will open. As usual, Git even explains how all that works:

```
 1  pick 98ec667 Implemented subtraction for integers
 2  pick 7c51980 Implemented subtraction for doubles
 3  pick 70be161 Refactored the subtraction methods to \
 4  provide only one implementation for both type of pa\
 5  rameters
 6
 7  ## Rebase b4bdab6..70be161 onto b4bdab6 (3 commands)
 8  ##
 9  ## Commands:
10  ## p, pick <commit> = use commit
11  ## r, reword <commit> = use commit, but edit the co\
12  mmit message
13  ## e, edit <commit> = use commit, but stop for amen\
14  ding
15  ## s, squash <commit> = use commit, but meld into p\
16  revious commit
17  ## f, fixup <commit> = like "squash", but discard t\
18  his commit's log message
19  ## x, exec <command> = run command (the rest of the\
20   line) using shell
21  ## b, break = stop here (continue rebase later with\
22   'git rebase --continue')
23  ## d, drop <commit> = remove commit
24  ## l, label <label> = label current HEAD with a name
25  ## t, reset <label> = reset HEAD to a label
26  ## m, merge [-C <commit> | -c <commit>] <label> [# \
27  <oneline>]
28  ## .        create a merge commit using the original\
29   merge commit's
30  ## .        message (or the oneline, if no original \
31  merge commit was
32  ## .        specified). Use -c <commit> to reword th\
33  e commit message.
```

```
34  ##
35  ## These lines can be re-ordered; they are executed\
36   from top to bottom.
37  ##
```

So, the idea is to chose among the operations that are offered by Git to edit the top of the message. Before diving into the main operations Git offers in an interactive rebase, let's remember that rebasing changes the repository history, thus requiring extra care with already pushed commits.

Let's go through some of the commonly used operations here one by one.

Pick

As stated by Git, to `pick` a commit is to use it. That means we'll reapply the commit as-is, without modifying it. We'll see that the situation is usually a bit more nuanced than that, and that the actions performed on the following commits influence that a great deal.

Reword

There is not much to say about `reword` that's not been said by Git itself. It's like picking a commit, except that we'll have the chance to change the commit message.

Edit

The next one is `edit`, which is interesting because it allows us to bring some modifications to the content of a commit. Let's say we thought of some updates that should've been part of a previous commit, this is our chance to put them into that very commit.

Drop

This one's rather explicit, the idea is to not use the commit at all. Another way to do that is to remove the line of that commit in the editor.

Squash and Fixup

Finally, the `squash` and `fixup` operations. Let's start with squash, as once we grasp how it works, the other one will make sense right away.

So, Git says that squashing a commit is to combine it into the previous one. Let's imagine we chose to pick the first commit and squash the second, that way we'll have only one commit with the implementation of the methods (thus modifying the first commit).

Again, in the editor that popped up, we'll be prompted with `pick` for all new commits. Let's change some of these so that they're not all picked:

```
1  pick 98ec667 Implemented subtraction for integers
2  squash 7c51980 Implemented subtraction for doubles
3  pick 70be161 Refactored the subtraction methods to \
4  provide only one implementation for both type of pa\
5  rameters
```

Then we save and Git opens a new editor, offering us the chance to review the commit message of the combined commit that we've squashed together:

```
1   ## This is a combination of 2 commits.
2   ## This is the 1st commit message:
3
4   Implemented subtraction for integers
5
6   ## This is the commit message #2:
7
8   Implemented subtraction for doubles
```

We can see that, initially, Git keeps the messages of all the commits. We can change them, keep them or discard them - whatever we want.

Now, if we used fixup instead of squash, then the message of the second commit wouldn't have been picked by default.

Remember that rebasing may modify the commit history, thus requiring a forced push to update our remote branch.

We'll talk a bit more about squashing in the next chapter on good and bad practices!

Reorder

In addition to the proposed operations, there is one more thing we can do while interactively rebasing. We can change the order of the commits. For that, we've just got to move the line of a commit elsewhere in the list, remembering that the commits are applied top to bottom.

Interactive Staging

When staging files, so far, we've either been adding them one by one, by using the git add command, followed by the filename, all of them by using `git add .` or a subset of files fitting some pattern by using globs.

Similar to how we can interactively rebase, we can also interactively stage files. This process give you a fine-grained insight into what's being added. This is useful if you've been working for a long time, have a bunch of changes and forgot what you've added. Or, if you simply want to have another look so that you can give constructive messages in the commits.

Finally, you might want to break down some changes into multiple commits, perhaps.

In any of these cases, interactive staging is your friend, and you activate it with a simple -i flag.

Let's add a few files and some contents into them:

```
1  $ touch file1.txt
2  $ echo "Hello World!" >> file1.txt
3
4  $ touch file2.txt
5  $ echo "Hello Git!" >> file2.txt
6
7  $ touch file3.txt
8  $ echo "Lorem ipsum dolor sit amet" >> file3.txt
9  $ echo "consecteur adipiscing elit" >> file3.txt
```

Now, we've got three new files, each with some different contents. Usually, we'd add them to the staging area before committing them. This time around, let's add them with some more insight:

```
1  $ git add -i
2
3  *** Commands ***
4    1: status        2: update       3: revert        4\
5  : add untracked
6    5: patch         6: diff         7: quit          8\
7  : help
8  What now>
```

The command will give us a git status like list of tracked files and the changes in them. Since we haven't tracked any yet, let's use the add untracked command to add them. To use these commands, you just call the first character of that command or the associated number, and press enter.

The book's render (or if you've obtained the printed version) might not have these highlighted, though, your interactive terminal should.

Let's add these files with either a or 4:

```
1  What now> 4
2    1: file1.txt
3    2: file2.txt
4    3: file3.txt
```

Now, we get to select *which* files here we'd like to perform this action on. Let's say we want to track file1.txt, but not the other files. We'd enter 1:

```
1   Add untracked>> 1
2   * 1: file1.txt
3     2: file2.txt
4     3: file3.txt
```

Now, it's marked to be added. In the next prompt, without typing anything, just press enter, to exit the action's menu:

```
1   Add untracked>>
2   added 1 path
3
4   *** Commands ***
5     1: status      2: update      3: revert      4\
6   : add untracked
7     5: patch       6: diff        7: quit        8\
8   : help
9   What now>
```

Now, let's quit this menu and check what happened with git status:

```
1   What now> q
2   Bye.
3
4   $ git status
5   On branch main
6   Your branch is ahead of 'origin/main' by 4 commits.
7     (use "git push" to publish your local commits)
8
9   Changes to be committed:
10    (use "git restore --staged <file>..." to unstage)
11          new file:   file1.txt
```

```
12
13  Untracked files:
14    (use "git add <file>..." to include in what will \
15  be committed)
16          file2.txt
17          file3.txt
```

Great! Our file is added to the staging area. Let's explore some other commands:

```
1   $ git add -i
2             staged      unstaged path
3    1:        +1/-0        nothing file1.txt
4
5   *** Commands ***
6    1: status      2: update      3: revert      4\
7   : add untracked
8    5: patch       6: diff        7: quit        8\
9   : help
10  What now>
```

This time around, we've got a staged file, which is now shown in the list. There's nothing unstaged for that file, or rather, it's up-to-date.

Let's add the other two files and update the first one:

```
1   What now> 4
2     1: file2.txt
3     2: file3.txt
4   Add untracked>> 1, 2
5   * 1: file2.txt
6   * 2: file3.txt
7   Add untracked>>
8   added 2 paths
9
10  *** Commands ***
11    1: status        2: update        3: revert        4\
12  : add untracked
13    5: patch         6: diff          7: quit          8\
14  : help
15  What now>
```

When adding multiple files, you can add them as 1, 2 instead
of running the command multiple times.

Let's add some changes to the first file now:

```
1   What now> q
2   Bye.
3
4   $ echo "We're exploring interactive staging" >> fil\
5   e1.txt
6   $ git add -i
7              staged     unstaged path
8     1:       +1/-0        +1/-0 file1.txt
9     2:       +1/-0      nothing file2.txt
10    3:       +2/-0      nothing file3.txt
11
12  *** Commands ***
```

```
13   1: status        2: update       3: revert       4\
14  : add untracked
15   5: patch         6: diff         7: quit         8\
16  : help
17  What now>
```

Now, there's an unstaged change to the file1.txt which we haven't added yet. The other two files are just fine. We'll first want to add the change to this file, and then look at the diff between the original new file1.txt:

```
1   *** Commands ***
2    1: status        2: update       3: revert       4\
3   : add untracked
4    5: patch         6: diff         7: quit         8\
5   : help
6   # Update staged file
7   What now> 2
8            staged      unstaged path
9    1:       +1/-0        +1/-0 file1.txt
10  # Select file
11  Update>> 1
12           staged      unstaged path
13  * 1:      +1/-0        +1/-0 file1.txt
14  # Empty command to go back
15  Update>>
16  updated 1 path
17
18  *** Commands ***
19   1: status        2: update       3: revert       4\
20  : add untracked
21   5: patch         6: diff         7: quit         8\
22  : help
```

```
23  # Diff command
24  What now> 6
25                staged      unstaged path
26    1:          +2/-0       nothing file1.txt
27    2:          +1/-0       nothing file2.txt
28    3:          +2/-0       nothing file3.txt
29  # Select file
30  Review diff>> 1
31  diff --git a/file1.txt b/file1.txt
32  new file mode 100644
33  index 0000000..7ab19e2
34  --- /dev/null
35  +++ b/file1.txt
36  @@ -0,0 +1,2 @@
37  +Hello World!
38  +We're exploring interactive staging
39  *** Commands ***
40    1: status       2: update       3: revert        4\
41  : add untracked
42    5: patch        6: diff         7: quit          8\
43  : help
44  What now>
```

As usual, we've entered the diff menu and selected the file
we wish to inspect. Then, we've been prompted with the diff
for file1.txt, just as we'd call git diff file1.txt.

Let's add yet another line to file1.txt:

```
1  $ echo "The answer to life, the universe and everyt\
2  hing is" >> file1.txt
3  $ echo "42" >> file1.txt
```

Now, say we want to keep the "Hello World", "We're exploring interactive staging" and "42" additions, but *don't* want to keep the "The answer to life, the universe and everything is" addition. We can use the patch command to select only certain changes.

Let's do that now:

```
1   # Select menu
2   What now> 5
3                 staged      unstaged path
4     1:          +2/-0          +2/-0 file1.txt
5   # Select file
6   Patch update>> 1
7                 staged      unstaged path
8   * 1:          +2/-0          +2/-0 file1.txt
9   # Exit menu, we've selected the files we wish to pa\
10  tch
11  Patch update>>
12  diff --git a/file1.txt b/file1.txt
13  index 7ab19e2..bc7fb13 100644
14  --- a/file1.txt
15  +++ b/file1.txt
16  @@ -1,2 +1,4 @@
17   Hello World!
18   We're exploring interactive staging
19  +The answer to life, the universe and everything is
20  +42
21  (1/1) Stage this hunk [y,n,q,a,d,e,?]?
```

Now, we can see our two new changes. And we'd like to throw away the first one, leaving only 42 behind. Until you get used to this menu, you can ask for help to see what each of these commands do by putting in a question mark:

```
 1  (1/1) Stage this hunk [y,n,q,a,d,e,?]? ?
 2  y - stage this hunk
 3  n - do not stage this hunk
 4  q - quit; do not stage this hunk or any of the rema\
 5  ining ones
 6  a - stage this hunk and all later hunks in the file
 7  d - do not stage this hunk or any of the later hunk\
 8  s in the file
 9  e - manually edit the current hunk
10  ? - print help
11  @@ -1,2 +1,4 @@
12    Hello World!
13    We're exploring interactive staging
14  +The answer to life the universe and everything is
15  +42
16  (1/1) Stage this hunk [y,n,q,a,d,e,?]?
```

We'll go with e, as it'll let us manually edit the contents:

```
 1  (1/1) Stage this hunk [y,n,q,a,d,e,?]? e
```

And this opens up a text editor, in which we can manually edit and remove the line we don't want:

```
1   # Manual hunk edit mode -- see bottom for a quick g\
2   uide.
3   @@ -1,2 +1,4 @@
4    Hello World!
5    We're exploring interactive staging
6   +The answer to life the universe and everything is
7   +42
8   # ---
9   # To remove '-' lines, make them ' ' lines (context\
10  ).
11  # To remove '+' lines, delete them.
12  # Lines starting with # will be removed.
13  #
14  # If the patch applies cleanly, the edited hunk wil\
15  l immediately be
16  # marked for staging.
17  # If it does not apply cleanly, you will be given a\
18  n opportunity to
19  # edit again.  If all lines of the hunk are removed\
20  , then the edit is
21  # aborted and the hunk is left unchanged.
```

Git gives us some help here, telling us how to remove a line. Since we want to remove a + line, we'll just delete it. If we wanted to remove a - line, we'd turn it into ' '. Now, let's remove line:

```
1   # Manual hunk edit mode -- see bottom for a quick g\
2   uide.
3   @@ -1,2 +1,4 @@
4    Hello World!
5    We're exploring interactive staging
6   +42
7   # ---
8   # To remove '-' lines, make them ' ' lines (context\
9   ).
10  # To remove '+' lines, delete them.
11  # Lines starting with # will be removed.
12  #
13  # If the patch applies cleanly, the edited hunk wil\
14  l immediately be
15  # marked for staging.
16  # If it does not apply cleanly, you will be given a\
17  n opportunity to
18  # edit again.  If all lines of the hunk are removed\
19  , then the edit is
20  # aborted and the hunk is left unchanged.
```

And close the editor, saving the document. This will patch the contents, such that we no longer have that line staged:

```
1   *** Commands ***
2     1: status        2: update        3: revert        4\
3   : add untracked
4     5: patch         6: diff          7: quit          8\
5   : help
6   What now> 1
7               staged       unstaged path
8     1:        +3/-0          +1/-0 file1.txt
9     2:        +1/-0        nothing file2.txt
10    3:        +2/-0        nothing file3.txt
```

Now, we can commit this state of files:

```
1   $ git commit -m "Adding files - file1, file2 and fi\
2   le3, without erroneous line in file1"
```

And push those changes to remote:

```
1   $ git push
2   Enumerating objects: 18, done.
3   Counting objects: 100% (18/18), done.
4   Delta compression using up to 4 threads
5   Compressing objects: 100% (12/12), done.
6   Writing objects: 100% (15/15), 1.68 KiB | 430.00 Ki\
7   B/s, done.
8   Total 15 (delta 5), reused 1 (delta 1), pack-reused\
9   0
10  remote: Resolving deltas: 100% (5/5), completed wit\
11  h 3 local objects.
12  To https://github.com/dupirefr/calculator
13     c367c20..1e7583f  main -> main
```

And, on our remote, we can see that the change isn't committed, although the unstaged change is still present in our working directory:

9. Good/Bad Practices

We've gone through a lot so far - the basics of working with Git, working with branches and remote repositories, as well as some advanced operations. We've also covered a few standard ways to use Git on a collaborative project, and included some good practices there.

In all of these chapters, we've tried including notes and disclaimers about certain operations and how to use them responsibly. Such as, which files to include in the `.gitignore` vs `exclude` file, or which things to look out for when rebasing.

Now is the time for some general good and bad practices. This will be a more opinionated chapter, filled with the personal experience of the authors and the way they see things right now. They may change in the future, in the light of new knowledge. Be sure to take a step back after reading this chapter and decide for yourself if that makes sense.

Commit Often

What does committing often mean? That means our commits should be relatively small. That facilitates going back when making a mistake.

Let's consider our Calculator project. If we'd implemented all the operations in the same commit, and the fourth operation had a mistake in it. It would've been difficult to just roll back that mistake, or rather - it would be impossible. We'd have to roll back other features as well, which might be important for someone else to use.

We'd roll back 4 methods, just to work on one.

By committing more often, let's say at least one commit for each calculator operation here, then we are creating a safety nest that prevents us from having to roll back changes that are still good, or to remove the changes manually without using Git (which can be tedious and error-prone).

The frequency of commits depends largely on your project and the scope of changes you make to the files in it. There isn't a one-size-fits-all argument here where someone can say "commit every n changes!".

Be reasonable with the number of commits so that each contains related changes that make sense to roll back together.

Another example - you're working on a web application. You change something in the back end and wish to commit that change. But you also notice a typo on the front-end, that the user can see. You quickly fix this typo and commit the changes. Two birds with one stone!

Later on, you have to rework the back-end change you've made - but when you roll back, the front-end typo comes back! These should be totally unrelated commits, even though one of them is *extremely small*. Avoid mixing apples and oranges.

If the back-end change necessitates a change in the front-end as well, such as adding an element that shows the result of an operation in the back-end, then yes - it makes sense to commit them together. When you roll back, if need be, you'll remove this element from the front-end. If it wasn't removed, the removal of the back-end service could result in a broken UI for the end-user.

Write Meaningful Commit Messages

In addition to committing often, we should ensure our commits make sense. This is easier when committing often, but still we should take care that a commit doesn't contain changes in too many parts of the code at once.

Again, we want to prevent having to roll back changes that are good because we made a mistake elsewhere. In addition, meaningful commits make it easier for other people to understand what we've done. Especially if, in addition to taking care of the commit content, we're also using explicit commit messages!

Explicit commit messages give direct access to the meaning of the commit, what we tried to achieve within that commit.

For example, imagine you've just jumped into the branch of a colleague to check what they've been doing, since you're expected to continue working on a feature with them.

You run the `git log --oneline` command and see this:

```
1  git log --oneline
2  05a63d1 sync
3  c367c20 changed file
4  ba2c556 multiplication
5  3649cab remote repo explanation
6  c776831 new main class
7  225a7d7 Merge
8  0e5cddc decimal addition
9  ...
```

These are simplified and shortened messages of the commits we've been working on in the book. Even though *we've* done these, it's still hard to reconstruct the history of what's been going on...

`decimal addition` can mean anything from fixing a bug, to covering an edge case, to deleting or adding a feature.

On the other hand, we could follow a convention called Conventional Commits[32] which have the following structure:

```
1   <type>[optional scope]: <description>
2
3   [optional body]
4
5   [optional footer(s)]
```

This same set of commits could then look like this:

```
1   git log --oneline
2   05a63d1 Merge remote-tracking branch 'origin/main' \
3   into main
4   c367c20 docs: Added information about the project c\
5   ollaborators
6   ba2c556 feat: Added a feature to multiply integer a\
7   nd decimal number
8   3649cab docs: Added explanation about the remote re\
9   pository
10  c776831 feat: Added Application to call the Calcula\
11  tor
12  225a7d7 Merge branch 'feature/addition'
13  0e5cddc feat: Implemented decimal addition on a bra\
```

---

[32]https://www.conventionalcommits.org/en/v1.0.0/

```
14   nch
15   ...
```

You're free to follow any convention you'd like - but try to make it a habit of using explicit, meaningful commit messages that others will understand as well.

Rebase Often from the Main Branch

We should make sure our code doesn't rely on an obsolete codebase. Therefore, we should often rebase our branches on top of the principal branch (whether it is main, develop or something else).

What is often?

Probably *every day*.

We want to do that because it allows us to catch conflicts early. If we rebase each morning, then the encountered conflicts can't come further than from the day before. Then, they are easier to resolve. We can easily catch up with the developer that wrote the conflicting code, and decide with them how to resolve that conflict.

On the contrary, if we're working on a long-running branch, let's say a few months, and we never rebased - conflicts happening in the first commits of that branch won't be that easy to solve. The other developer might not remember what they did, nor why, just as you'll most probably forget the concrete small decisions you made months ago. They might even not be working on that project anymore!

You might also wonder why *rebase* and not *merge*? Rebase keeps the history clean. This way, there are no merge commits, which pollute the history and make history visualization cumbersome.

If you use a graphical tool for visualization, you'd notice the merges all around the place. A simple visualization tool, built-in to Git can be accessed via the git log command, and using the --graph flag:

```
$ git log --graph
*   commit 05a63d102a8613e2cb986e59e52042b485976d1e\
(HEAD -> main)
|\  Merge: c367c20 ba2c556
| | Author: francois <francois.dupire@nerthusconsul\
ting.be>
| | Date:   Sun Dec 13 21:04:10 2020 +0100
| |
| |     Merge remote-tracking branch 'origin/main' \
into main
| |
| * commit ba2c55672e57cb8311dd2e1ddf21500e62498484
| | Author: collaborator <francois.dupire@nerthusco\
nsulting.be>
| | Date:   Sun Dec 13 20:56:09 2020 +0100
| |
| |     Added a feature to multiply integer and dec\
imal number
| |
* | commit c367c20ff684e5486fd50cd19ed4182f033612c2
|/  Author: francois <francois.dupire@nerthusconsul\
ting.be>
|   Date:   Sun Dec 13 21:01:01 2020 +0100
|
```

```
25  |        Added information about the project collabo\
26  rators
27  |
28  * commit 3649cab5194c5b453c8bae5129dd740f52d51694
29  | Author: francois <francois.dupire@nerthusconsulti\
30  ng.be>
31  | Date:   Sun Dec 13 20:42:21 2020 +0100
32  |
33  |        Added explanation about the remote repository
34  |
35  * commit c776831d3eb07fb5da65d6bd729b787c5aea16d6
36  | Author: francois <francois.dupire@nerthusconsulti\
37  ng.be>
38  | Date:   Fri Dec 11 07:59:15 2020 +0100
39  |
40  |        Added Application to call the Calculator
41  |
42  :
```

On a simple project like this, there isn't much to be visualized, but you get the point.

Plus, all of our commits are stay packed together on top of our branch. That is also cleaner, but will be useful for squashing (see below).

Don't Rebase the Main Branch

On the other hand, while we want to rebase *from* the main/develop branch frequently, we don't want to alter the history of the main/develop branch itself.

Exactly in the spirit of other people rebasing from it frequently, any change to the history of main can introduce a myriad of conflicts for everyone else, that's rebasing from it. Once it's made it to the `main/develop` branch and time has passed, you've missed your time to refactor it.

Think about refactoring things ahead - interactively rebase your branches before submitting for a code review, squash commits together, tag them, fix errors, etc.

Don't Commit Generated Files

Generated files, such as logs or IDE-related files, are generally left uncommitted and untracked. This, in some cases comes down to personal preferences, but in general, you'll see some consensus as to which files to avoid:

- System files (i.e. Mac's `.DS_Store`)
- App configuration files (i.e. `app.config`, `.env`, etc.)
- Build artifacts (i.e. `*.pyc`)
- Installed dependencies (i.e. `node_modules`)
- Non-documentation and personal text files (i.e. `todo.txt`)
- Application data and logs (i.e. `*.log`, `*.sqlite`, etc.)
- Dev configuration files (i.e. `.jshintrc`)
- Generated or minified source code (i.e. `*.min.js`)

From developer to developer, this list will be different, though, some these are some of the things that are very generally not committed.

Push Often

We never know what can go on in our lives. We can drop our laptop, have our hard disk crash because of heavy usage, a fire may occur in the office!

In case of a fire, instead of writing:

```
1  $ git commit -m "FIRE"
2  $ git push
```

And then running out off the building, keep your work backed up and frequently updated. To ensure that, we should push often. Then, let's remember that we should either push on a branch or push code that is safe-to-go in production - by using feature toggle as we've seen before, if the features aren't ready yet.

Again, often should be at least once a day so that in the *worst-case* scenario, you lose a day's worth of work.

Squash Before Going on the Main Branch

Now, we did say "create small commits", and no, it doesn't go against this advice. Small commits are for organizing your work and to facilitate rolling back when needed. When you want to merge your work back into the `main` branch (or `develop`), you don't want to drown everyone's work (including your own) with 100 commits. Also, when someone's doing code review, they'll want to view more than just the small changes.

Additionally, there are often automated builds and tests that check the sanity of the main branch of the remote repository. Imagine we break those with our work, and we don't have time to investigate right now.

What do we do?

It's easy! We covered that in the previous chapter: a `revert` will allow us to remove the erroneous code with ease, without losing anything in the process so that we can fix it at a later time! Also, you pushed 50 commits, and one (or ten) of those cause the issue. Reverting doesn't seem that great anymore...

If we squashed those fifty commits into one (or even two or three) - then reverting is a piece of cake! We won't be able to roll back some specific pieces of our code anymore, but at this stage we should have pretty solid work and don't need to do that anymore. That was mainly useful during the development stage.

A balance between these two is important, and it's something that depends on your project, the way you personally do things and the speed of development.

Also, we prefer the `squash` operation, instead of `fixup`. Conserving the commit messages in the squashed commit messages is important to keep a trace of the work that's been done. It'll be easier for collaborators to understand the different steps we went through, and maybe get a good idea of what we've achieved exactly, without having to read all the code.

Don't Cherry-Pick Often

One last thing is to avoid cherry-picking. It can really lead to cumbersome situations and shouldn't be used, at least not often. There will be times when it's difficult to avoid it, but whenever possible we should rely on other Git mechanisms.

As we've seen, a new hash is created for the commit created by a cherry-pick, thus making the two commits totally unrelated. In the article series mentioned in the previous chapter, the author even illustrates how some changes can be totally lost by using cherry-picks, without a conflict even being raised by Git.

Cherry-picking requires extensive attention from everyone on board, and oftentimes leads to issues, so we should really be careful when using the operation, and if possible, avoid it altogether!